FOR THE

LOVE

OF

POPSICLES

FOR THE

LOVE

OF

POPSICLES

NATURALLY DELICIOUS ICY SWEET SUMMER TREATS FROM A–Z

SARAH BOND
CREATOR OF LIVE EAT LEARN

Skyhorse Publishing

Skyhorse Publishing books may be purchased in bulk at special discounts for sales promotion, corporate gifts, fund-raising, or educational purposes. Special editions can also be created to specifications. For details, contact the Special Sales Department, Skyhorse Publishing, 307 West 36th Street, 11th Floor, New York, NY 10018 or info@skyhorsepublishing.com.

Skyhorse® and Skyhorse Publishing® are registered trademarks of Skyhorse Publishing, Inc.®, a Delaware corporation.

Visit our website at www.skyhorsepublishing.com.

10 9 8

Library of Congress Cataloging-in-Publication Data

Names: Bond, Sarah, author.
Title: For the love of popsicles : naturally delicious icy sweet summer
   treats from A-Z / Sarah Bond.
Description: New York City : Skyhorse Publishing, [2019]
Identifiers: LCCN 2018054403| ISBN 9781510741973 (hardcover : alk. paper) |
   ISBN 9781510742017 (ebook)
Subjects: LCSH: Ice pops. | Desserts. | Cookbooks.
Classification: LCC TX796.I46 B66 2019 | DDC 641.86--dc23 LC record available at https://lccn.loc.gov/2018054403

Cover design by Qualcom
Cover photograph by Sarah Bond
Author photographs by Molly Bond
All other photographs by Sarah Bond

Print ISBN: 978-1-5107-4197-3
Ebook ISBN: 978-1-5107-4201-7

Printed in China

To my family for believing in me,
Jor for inspiring me, and the readers of
Live Eat Learn who made it all possible.

A Note on Contents

This popsicle-pedia is organized completely from A to Z! But if you've got a certain craving, refer to these helpful categories to find your recipe.

INTRODUCTION

A Love Affair with Popsicles

I have a tendency to collect too many kitchen gadgets and food props, despite living in a typically tiny Dutch house in the Netherlands. And among my spiralizers, sushi mats, and other long forgotten kitchen tools sat my popsicle mold, collecting dust. When I'd bought the mold, all the popsicle recipes I could find relied on copious amounts of sugar, heavy cream, or sweetened condensed milk as key ingredients, none of which I was particularly comfortable using. Having grown up in a healthyish home and studying nutrition and dietetics in college, the thought of snacking on a frozen bar of sweetened condensed milk was enough to make my belly churn. So, I came to believe that popsicles were inherently unhealthy, and the popsicle mold gathered dust.

But there's one thing they don't tell you about summers in the Netherlands. They're hot. And the closest thing to air conditioning is standing in front of a freezer with the door open. So I dug out the dusty popsicle mold in a last-ditch effort to cool my bones, spooning in a simple combo of honey-sweetened Greek yogurt. The result was creamy smooth deliciousness that was subtly sweet and surprisingly healthy! I began experimenting with various popsicle bases, like coconut milk and fresh fruit, and with each successful batch became more confident in the power of the popsicle to be a healthy way of beating the heat (a.k.a. I could eat four pops in a day without an ounce of guilt).

As my love affair with the popsicle mold blossomed, so did the world's love of popsicles. Artisanal popsicle shops were sprouting up in cities around the world, touting wide selections and unique flavor combinations. I wanted to share just how easy these treats were to make at home, so I began sharing my popsicle recipe creations on my vegetarian food blog, Live Eat Learn. But with more popsicle ideas than I could reasonably post online, this cookbook, *For the Love of Popsicles*, was born.

About the Recipes

The popsicle recipes in this book are intended to be wholesome and approachable. By "wholesome" I generally mean the recipes are healthier than your average pop, using down-to-earth ingredients and ranging from just 16 calories (in the Rainbow Fruit Pops, page 131) to 219 calories (in the Mint Chocolate Pops, page 97).

We'll use rich Greek yogurt and coconut milk in lieu of heavy cream or condensed milk, and use at least half the amount of added sweetener found in traditional homemade pops (we'll typically use ¼ cup per batch, as compared to the ½ cup found in traditional recipes). We'll also use easy-to-find unrefined sugars, like honey and maple syrup, which add natural sweetness and rounder flavor than refined sugar. On the topic of flavor, fresh fruits, herbs, spices, and citrus zests will take the place of extracts and artificial flavors to create pops that rival the old classics (with a few fun flavor combos, like Pineapple Basil (page 119), thrown in).

In terms of approachability, ingredients are tailored to be easily found in your neighborhood grocery store or farmers' market. Many of the recipes require you to simply blend the ingredients, pour into molds, and freeze. But of course, I want to show you the world of pop-ssibilities so some recipes will be more involved—like layering, for example. I've included a difficulty level with each recipe to help you know what to expect (but remember, I'll be guiding you the whole way!).

Not much is worse than spending time and money on a recipe only for it to tremendously flop. I was committed

 Easy—simple tasks such as blending or stirring

 Involved—additional steps such as cooking or layering

Difficult—complex techniques such as whipping meringue

to creating popsicle recipes that work for *real* people in *real* kitchens, so I enlisted the help of taste testers to ensure each recipe in this book works for you. Fifteen women and their families, from Alaska to Florida, spent the summer testing and helping to refine these recipes to be as delicious as possible. Meet the tasters on page 164.

HOMEMADE   STOREBOUGHT

The Basics of Popsicle Making

IT'S NOT ROCKET SCIENCE

In my first week of college I walked into what I thought was my Intro to Engineering course, only to come to the slow and dreadful realization that I was indeed sitting in Space Propulsion and Physics . . . rocket science. I immediately ran in the opposite direction, eventually finding myself in the field of food and nutrition. Delicious, approachable, and decidedly *not* rocket science. Coincidentally, I would use the same words to describe popsicle making!

In fact, making your own popsicles is virtually foolproof. There are, of course, some fundamentals to achieving the perfectly textured pop, which we'll get into later in this section. But by simply tasting the mixture before freezing, you'll have an idea of what to expect from the finished pops and can adjust as needed. Given that your ingredients may differ depending on brand or seasonality (such as sweetness differences in fruits), these recipes should be considered as guidelines. Always taste the popsicle mixture before freezing and adjust as needed. Here's a quick guide to get your perfect taste:

- Too sweet? Add sourness, like lemon or lime juice
- Too sour? Add sweetness, like honey or maple syrup
- Too bitter? Add creaminess, like yogurt or coconut milk, or add sweetness
- Too salty? Add sweet and sourness

Keep in mind that when you freeze the popsicles, they will taste less intense than the unfrozen mixture. A strongly flavored mixture makes for perfectly flavored pops!

FREEZING

You've arrived at your ideal popsicle mixture and it's time to freeze! Here are some things to keep in mind when transforming this glorified smoothie into a gourmet pop:

Allow room for expansion: Pour or spoon the mixture into your popsicle molds, leaving about ¼ inch free at the top to allow room for them to expand. Tap your mold firmly on the counter to remove air bubbles.

Crooked sticks: You may have trouble getting your popsicle sticks to stand upright, depending on the recipe and your popsicle mold. To fix this, freeze the pops for 1 hour, or until slightly thickened, then insert sticks and freeze until solid. Alternatively, cover the popsicle mold firmly with aluminum foil and pierce popsicle sticks through the foil and into the pops. The aluminum foil should help keep the sticks in place.

Freeze time: Depending on the thickness of your mold, most pops should freeze in 4 to 6 hours. Boozy pops will require longer freezing times, at least 8 hours.

Freezing speed: The speed at which your popsicles freeze will impact the final texture. When pops freeze quickly, there is less time for ice crystals to form, meaning the popsicles will be softer and creamier. For this reason, industrial-scale popsicle makers freeze their pops in minutes using ultra-cold alcohol baths and blast freezers. You can achieve similar results at home with fast-freezing molds, like those made by Zoku. Otherwise, simply setting your freezer to its coldest temperature and placing pops near the back will make for faster freezing. Every recipe in this book was developed to work in the average kitchen, using simple molds in a home freezer. Freezing the pops faster will therefore only be an improvement to these already tried, tested, and well-loved recipes.

UNMOLDING

I've found the easiest way of unmolding pops is to run them under a faucet of warm water, moving the mold around constantly so that each popsicle well is under the water for a few seconds. Try to run water only on the molds, avoiding the tops. Gently tug the sticks. If pops don't come out fairly easily, return to the water briefly. If pops are soft when they come out of the molds, set them on a plate and return to the freezer until solid. An alternative method for unmolding is to fill your sink with warm water and briefly dunk the mold in the water, though I've found this method takes much more water and time.

STORING

Fresh ingredients and no preservatives mean these homemade pops won't last as long as the store-bought kind, but that's not to say you can't keep a few varieties in the freezer for when the summer sweet tooth hits. Remove popsicles from their molds and store in resealable freezer bags or airtight freezer containers. They will taste best if eaten within 4 to 6 weeks of making them.

HOW TO CREATE LAYERS

Layers add pizzazz to pops and are easy to make, albeit slightly more time-consuming—but they are so worth it! Blend each of the layers separately, cleaning out the blender between each batch. For layers where there is a small amount of mixture to blend, it may be easier to use either a small or handheld immersion blender.

Clean layers: For crisp, unblended layers, freeze each layer completely before pouring in the next. A spouted measuring cup will help you pour cleanly and evenly into each well. Use a paper towel to wipe any drips on the inside, then insert popsicle sticks. Sticks may have a hard time standing upright when freezing the first layer.

To solve this, tightly cover the top of the mold with aluminum foil and poke popsicle sticks through the foil and into the first layer. Freeze until solid, then repeat the process of pouring and freezing for remaining layers.

Blended layers: For layers that are slightly blended together, pour in the first layer then gently spoon the following layer on top, repeating for all layers. If your mixture is on the liquidy side, place an upside-down spoon just over the first layer and trickle the next layer over the spoon so that it slowly pours onto the first layer.

Supplies

POPSICLE MOLDS

With a rise in the world's love of popsicles has come a tidal wave of choices when it comes to choosing your mold. There are generally two types: classic and fast-freezing. The classic molds involve simply pouring in a mixture, inserting sticks, and freezing (usually for 4 to 6 hours). They come in a variety of shapes and materials from metal to silicone to BPA-free plastic. For best results, aim for skinnier molds as opposed to thicker. These will freeze faster and therefore have a softer texture.

The leveled-up version of the classic molds are fast-freezing molds like those sold by Zoku, which freeze pops within 10 minutes. With these molds, you chill the base unit overnight in the freezer, then simply pour in your mixture and watch it quickly freeze. A fast freeze time means these pops will have a softer texture, though these molds can come at a slightly higher price point. Every recipe in this book was tested and perfected with the classic-style popsicle mold, so fast freezing is not absolutely necessary for delicious pops!

Each recipe in this book makes about 16 ounces (2 cups), unless otherwise noted. This should give you eight 2-oz. pops or five 3.2-oz. pops.

No mold? No problem! You can make an assortment of pops with the supplies you probably already have in your kitchen, such as: tall glasses, small yogurt containers, ice cube trays, shot glasses, muffin tins, or disposable paper cups. You can even double your popsicle mix and pour it into a plastic wrap-lined loaf pan! Cover the pan with foil, poke sticks through, and freeze, then simply slice and serve.

OTHER USEFUL SUPPLIES

Aside from the mold, there are a few other common kitchen gadgets that will come in handy in your popsicle making:

Countertop or handheld blender: Using a good quality blender is the first step in most popsicle recipes. My love affair with popsicles is rivaled only by my love for the Vitamix, which pulverizes just about anything into smooth perfection. For smaller batches, the Nutribullet will also do the job.

Spouted glass measuring cup: Makes for easy measuring and clean pouring into narrow molds.

Microplane zester: Fresh citrus zest lends loads of flavor to fruity pops without the added sourness. A microplane will be your secret weapon in these recipes.

Measuring spoons: For the little things.

Mesh sieve: Fresh fruits, unlike ready-made juices, contains skins and seeds. For the times when we want to keep those out of our pops, a wire mesh sieve will be our simple solution.

Resealable bags or airtight freezer containers: To ward off freezer burn and keep your pops fresh.

Ingredients

At the heart of every good ice pop are quality ingredients making it all pop-ssible (sorry, this won't be the last popsi-pun). The ingredients in this book aim to strike the ever-tricky balance between "good tasting" and "good for you," while also being easy to find in your local grocery or farmers' market. Let's talk about those ingredients.

LAY THE BASE

The base ingredients play the pivotal role of determining whether you'll be gnawing on an ice block or relishing in soft popsicle bliss.

After testing out many ingredients to use as a base for creamy popsicles, full-fat Greek yogurt and canned coconut milk consistently produced the most velvety pops. As opposed to plain yogurt, Greek yogurt has more of the liquidy whey removed, meaning this yogurt is thicker, richer in protein, and makes for less icy popsicles. Full-fat canned coconut milk is another key player in many of these recipes. Keep in mind that this is *not* the watered down coconut milk found in a carton in the refrigerator section of the grocery, but rather the thick milk usually found in a 14-oz can. Using a whole milk variety of both the yogurt and coconut milk further adds biteable softness to your pops, whereas non-fat varieties may be icier.

Popsicles with a fruity base typically rely on fresh fruit purees, with the natural fibers adding softness to finished pops. Aim for fruits that are very ripe or even overripe as these will be the sweetest. You can often find mushy, soon-to-go-bad fruits at the farmers' market on discount. They may be unsightly but they'll make the best pops! If the season doesn't allow for fresh fruit, frozen will also work. Be sure to thaw the fruit before blending (quicken this up by setting the frozen fruit in a bowl and setting the bowl in warm water, making sure the water doesn't get onto the fruit).

SWEETEN IT UP

Not only is sugar a tasty addition to popsicles, it's a necessary one. Sugar molecules disrupt the formation of ice crystals which would otherwise turn your popsicle into a rock-hard block. In this book we'll mostly use unrefined liquid sugars, like honey and maple syrup, which add sweetness and flavor.

Many traditional popsicle recipes call for simple syrup, which is made from dissolving one part sugar in one part water. While you may use it as a sweetener if you'd like, the recipes in this book do not call for it. Not only does the making of simple syrup add an additional step in the popsicle making process, it doesn't provide the naturally flavorful or health-promoting polyphenol compounds found in honey, maple syrup, or agave nectar.

Each recipe is written using the best sweetener for that particular popsicle, but you're welcome to substitute it with your favorite sweetening ingredient. Because the texture of pops often relies on sugar to prevent ice crystal formation, no-calorie sweeteners will not work well in most recipes. You'll find a note in the recipes where a no-calorie sweetener substitute is possible.

GET BOOZY

Of all the ingredients that prevent the dreaded ice block popsicle, alcohol is the champion for making delicate, flaky textured pops (a.k.a. poptails!). Most alcohols don't freeze well in a home freezer, so to ensure your mixture freezes into popsicles, be sure to keep the ratio of mixer to alcohol around 4:1 while avoiding strong liquors (> 20% ABV). Poptails will melt more quickly than your average pop, so leave them in the freezer until right before serving.

Tip: Not sure which apples to use? For sweeter pops use Gala, Fuji, Golden Delicious, or Honeycrisp. For a touch of sourness try Granny Smith or Pink Lady.

All-American Apple Pie

In a book full of our favorite popsicle classics, we obviously have to start with a pop inspired by the ultimate all-American dessert . . . apple pie! With spiced apple compote sandwiched between layers of creamy yogurt, these pops are perfect for filling the apple pie-less void known as summertime.

difficulty   **Yields: about 2 cups, 8 (2-oz.) pops**

1 large apple, cored and finely chopped (peel can stay on)
4 Tbsp maple syrup, divided
2 Tbsp almond butter
2 Tbsp water
½ tsp ground cinnamon
Pinch of salt
1 cup plain Greek yogurt
½ tsp vanilla extract

1. Add apple, 2 tablespoons of the maple syrup, almond butter, water, cinnamon, and salt to a small saucepan. Cook over medium heat for 8 to 10 minutes, stirring occasionally, until apples have softened and resemble chunky applesauce. Set aside to cool to room temperature (quicken this up by setting the pan of apples in a sink full of cold water).

2. In a separate bowl, stir together remaining 2 tablespoons maple syrup, yogurt, and vanilla.

3. Spoon some of the yogurt mixture into each mold, followed by a bit of the apple mixture, followed by more yogurt. Continue adding each, in alternating layers, until you've used it all. Gently tap the pop mold on the counter to remove air pockets. Insert sticks and freeze until hard (at least 4 hours).

4. Run the mold under warm water for a few seconds to loosen them up, then remove from the mold.

Calories 94   **Fat** 4.1 g   **Saturated Fat** 1.3 g   **Carbs** 13.3 g   **Fiber** 1.2 g   **Sugar** 10.9 g   **Protein** 2.1 g

Almond Butter Maple

We've all had that moment when the magnetic force pulling you towards the jar of nut butter results in you scooping out a big glob, to be eaten off the spoon, obviously (no? just me?). Well these popsicles are the *sophisticated adult* version of that. Two seemingly simple ingredients, almond butter and maple syrup, converge into creamy pop greatness. It's like a spoon full of nut butter . . . but better.

difficulty   **Yields: about 2 cups, 8 (2-oz.) pops**

1 cup plain Greek yogurt
½ cup almond butter
1 banana
¼ cup maple syrup
½ tsp ground cinnamon

1. Combine all ingredients in a blender until smooth.

2. Pour into molds, leaving a little space at the top for them to expand. Insert sticks and freeze until hard (at least 4 hours).

3. Run the mold under warm water for a few seconds to loosen them up, then remove from the mold.

Calories 165   **Fat:** 10.8 g   **Saturated Fat** 1.9 g   **Carbs** 15 g   **Fiber** 2.1 g   **Sugar** 10.2 g   **Protein** 4.7 g

Amaretto Sour

I'm not known for my cocktails. Unless by "known" you mean the time in college when I made a jungle juice so sweet and strong that party-goers threw the stuff out the window. But there's one foolproof cocktail I can really get on board with—Amaretto Sours! This is usually a simple combination of lemon juice, amaretto liqueur, and sugar. To ice pop-ify it, we'll add just enough orange juice to freeze the mixture (and the natural sweetness will also reduce the amount of added sugar these pops need).

difficulty   **Yields: a bit over 2 cups, 8 (2-oz.) pops**

1 cup orange juice
½ cup amaretto liqueur (like Disaronno)
½ cup fresh lemon juice (3 lemons)
¼ cup honey

1. Stir together all ingredients, mixing well to evenly combine with the honey.

2. Pour into molds, leaving a little space at the top for them to expand. Insert sticks and freeze until hard (at least 8 hours). If sticks have a hard time standing straight up, let freeze for about 1 hour, then insert sticks.

3. Run the mold under warm water *very briefly* to loosen them up, then remove from the mold.

Calories 104   **Fat** 0.2 g   **Saturated Fat** 0.1 g   **Carbs** 20.8 g   **Fiber** 0.2 g   **Sugar** 13.1 g   **Alcohol** 3 g   **Protein** 0.4 g

Any Juice

Perhaps the most refreshingly simple promise of a popsicle mold is your ability to put plain ol' juice in and have any flavor of frozen treat come out. But while freezing pure juice would usually result in icy blocks, the simple addition of chopped fruit adds texture and fiber, making for a softer, even fruitier pop!

difficulty **Yields: about 2 cups, 8 (2-oz.) pops**

Choice of:
1½ cups orange juice with ½ cup segmented mandarins
1½ cups strawberry or pomegranate juice with ½ cup chopped strawberries
1½ cups pineapple juice with ½ cup chopped pineapple
1½ cups grape juice with ½ cup grapes

1. Chop up whichever fruit you're using and evenly distribute into the bottom of each well.

2. Pour in the juice, leaving a little space at the top for them to expand. Insert sticks and freeze until hard (at least 4 hours). If mixture is too liquidy for sticks to stand straight up, let freeze for about 1 hour, then insert sticks.

3. Run the mold under warm water for a few seconds to loosen them up, then remove from the mold.

Tip: *Nutrition information will differ depending on the juice you use, though the nutritional value for 8 ice pops should be about equal to 2 cups of juice (see the back of your juice package for the nutrition information).*

Tip: Lemon juice is a key ingredient in this recipe, so be sure to use fresh juice (not the bottled stuff) to avoid off-flavors.

Arnold Palmer

I don't know much about Arnold Palmer, or golf, or even iced tea, for that matter. But I do know that when the three converged, the simple drink come to be known as the Arnold Palmer was born. Named after the golfer who dreamed it up, this is a simple combination of lemonade and iced tea. And while you could throw sweet tea and lemonade into a mold and call it a day, we're using fresh brewed tea and lemon juice (plus zest) to make stronger-flavored pops that will help the flavors shine through when frozen!

difficulty    Yields: about 2 cups, 8 (2-oz.) pops

1¾ cups boiling water
¼ cup honey or sugar (taste and add more as needed)
3 bags black tea
¼ cup fresh lemon juice (1½ lemons)
2 Tbsp finely grated lemon zest (2 lemons)

1. Combine hot water and honey, stirring to dissolve. Add tea and let steep tea for 5 minutes before removing tea bags.

2. Add lemon juice and zest to the tea and allow to cool to lukewarm (quicken this up by setting the bowl/cup of hot tea in a sink full of cold water). Taste and add more sugar as needed to suit your taste.

3. Pour into molds, leaving a little space at the top for them to expand. Insert sticks and freeze until hard (at least 4 hours). If mixture is too liquidy for sticks to stand straight up, let freeze for about 1 hour, then insert sticks.

4. Run the mold under warm water for a few seconds to loosen them up, then remove from the mold.

Calories 27   **Fat** 0.1 g   **Saturated Fat** 0.1 g   **Carbs** 6.9 g   **Fiber** 0.1 g   **Sugar** 6.5 g   **Protein** 0.1 g

Avocado Chocolate

Have you ever wondered why we suddenly became infatuated with avocados? Well, there used to be a ban on fruits from Mexico (birthplace of the avocado) to America. When these import restrictions were loosened in the 90's and finally removed in 2007, avocados could flow freely into our country (and mouths). Top that with the early 2000's love of low carb, high fat diets and you have the makings for a generation that's gone avocontrol.

difficulty   **Yields: about 2 cups, 8 (2-oz.) pops**

1 ripe avocado, seeded and peeled
2 bananas
¾ cup milk (can substitute dairy-free)
2 Tbsp unsweetened cocoa powder
2 Tbsp packed brown sugar (can substitute no-calorie sweetener)

1. Combine all ingredients in a blender until smooth.
2. Pour into molds, leaving a little space at the top for them to expand. Insert sticks and freeze until hard (at least 4 hours).
3. Run the mold under warm water for a few seconds to loosen them up, then remove from the mold.

Calories 101   **Fat** 5.7 g   **Saturated Fat** 1.4 g   **Carbs** 13 g   **Fiber** 2.9 g   **Sugar** 7 g   **Protein** 1.8 g

Tip: *You'll know your avocado is ripe when you peel back the small stem on top and it is both easy to remove and green underneath. An underripe avocado will have a stem that's difficult to remove, while an overripe avocado will be brown under the stem.*

Tip: These pops are great for parties and gatherings! Arrange a bunch of different toppings in bowls with spoons for sprinkling, and melt a larger amount of chocolate than this recipe calls for (1½ to 2 cups) for easier and faster dipping.

Banana Choose Your Own Adventure

If ever there were a choose-your-own-adventure ice pop, it would be these banana pops. Like a blank canvas of chocola-tunity, they're just awaiting your culinary inspiration (or whatever seeds and sprinkles you happen to have in your pantry). The key to these pops is in the French method, mise-en-place, meaning "everything in its place." When the molten chocolate hits that frozen banana base it will solidify within 10 or so seconds, making it important to have your toppings all chopped and arranged nearby for quick and easy sprinkling!

difficulty   **Yields: 8 banana pops**

2 bananas, cut in half lengthwise and widthwise, so you have 8 pieces
¼ cup toppings, such as:
   Sprinkles
   Chopped nuts or seeds
   Shredded or shaved coconut
   Cocoa powder
   ½ cup dark or milk chocolate (chips or a roughly chopped bar)

1. Lay banana pieces flat side down and gently insert the stick about an inch or two into the banana, taking care not to go too far because the banana will crack. Set on a parchment paper–lined sheet or plate and freeze until hard (at least 2 hours).

2. Right before taking banana pops out of the freezer, prepare your toppings. Chop (if necessary) all desired toppings and place in bowls.

3. Melt the chocolate by adding it to a heat-resistant bowl. Bring a small pot of water to a boil and set the bowl of chocolate over the boiling water (just above the water, not submerged). Stir constantly until most of the chocolate is melted. Remove the bowl from over the steam and continue to stir until all chocolate has melted.

4. To assemble, dip bananas in the chocolate, using a spoon as needed to get it nice and coated. Working very quickly, coat in your desired toppings and let harden completely (just a minute or two).

Nutrition information will differ depending on your toppings. The following nutritional values are an indication of the bananas and chocolate, without toppings.

Calories 82   **Fat** 3.2 g   **Saturated Fat** 2.2 g   **Carbs** 13 g   **Fiber** 1.1 g   **Sugar** 9 g   **Protein** 1.1 g

Tip: Peach skins can be a love or hate thing, so either peel them before chopping, use a strong blender to pulverize the skins, or pour the blended mixture through a mesh sieve to remove large pieces of skin.

Bellini

If it were up to me, there would be no ice cubes. When they're not taking up space in your drink that could have otherwise been filled with more drink, they're melting your beverage into watery sadness. Frozen juice or pieces of fruit make for flavorful ice cubes, but if you're looking to step it up a refreshingly cold notch you can use popsicles! Peach pops play the role of ice cubes + fruit flavor bombs + drink stirrers in this classic(ish) Bellini cocktail.

difficulty

Yields: about 2 cups peach mixture, 8 (2-oz.) pops

6 peaches, chopped (optionally peeled first; see Tip)
1 Tbsp lemon juice (½ of a lemon)
2 Tbsp honey or sugar
1 750-mL bottle chilled prosecco

1. Combine peaches, lemon juice, and sweetener in a blender until smooth (optionally straining out peach skins with a mesh sieve if you didn't peel them).

2. Pour into molds, leaving a little space at the top for them to expand. Insert sticks and freeze until hard (at least 4 hours).

3. Run the mold under warm water for a few seconds to loosen them up, then remove from the mold.

4. Place popsicles individually into wine glasses or champagne flutes. Top with prosecco and serve.

Calories 115 **Fat** 0 g **Saturated Fat** 0 g **Carbs** 14.2 g **Fiber** 1.5 g **Sugar** 11.1 g **Alcohol** 8.5 g **Protein** 0.8 g

Blackberry Orange Basil

I cannot remember when the realization struck me that basil works with fruit, but a groundbreaking realization it was. Because basil doesn't just work with fruit. It is, to put it frankly, awesome with fruit. Tart flavors, like blackberries and orange, balance out the sweet inklings of basil, making for a pop that's more than meets the mouth.

difficulty

Yields: a bit over 2 cups, 8 (2-oz.) pops
(this is if you strain out the seeds; yields more if you leave them in)

3 cups blackberries (fresh or frozen and thawed)
1½ cups orange juice
½ cup loosely packed fresh basil (dried basil will *not* work well in this recipe)
3 Tbsp honey

1. Combine all ingredients in a blender until smooth (optionally straining out blackberry seeds with a mesh sieve).

2. Pour into molds, leaving a little space at the top for them to expand. Insert sticks and freeze until hard (at least 4 hours).

3. Run the mold under warm water for a few seconds to loosen them up, then remove from the mold.

Calories 69   **Fat** 0.4 g   **Saturated Fat** 0 g   **Carbs** 16.6 g   **Fiber** 3 g   **Sugar** 13 g   **Protein** 1.1 g

Tip: To remove the blackberry seeds, push the blended mixture through a fine mesh sieve using a rubber spatula. This is totally optional, but gives you a smoother pop!

Tip: The Bloody Mary is often served with celery to help cool off that spicy heat. While the ice pops by nature will certainly help, you can step it up a notch by using celery stalks in place of the wooden sticks!

Bloody Mary

Bloody Marys are the cocktail of possibility. Anyone who has had the privilege of visiting a Bloody Mary bar will understand. Like, is it breakfast? Sure, why not. Can I put a skewer of cheese and shrimp in it? Heck yeah! Throw a cheeseburger on top? Absolutely! Bloody Marys are a judgment-free zone. Which is why they also make the greatest ice pops! Icy coolness tames the flames, while the vodka gives these pops the perfectly soft frozen consistency. Settle into your summer (mornings) the right way.

difficulty   **Yields: about 2 cups, 8 (2-oz.) pops**

1½ cups tomato juice
⅓ cup vodka
1 Tbsp lime juice (½ of a lime)
1 tsp Worcestershire sauce
½–1 tsp Tabasco sauce, to taste
1 clove garlic, minced
¼ tsp salt
¼ tsp smoked paprika
Pinch of ground black pepper

1. Whisk together all ingredients, adding more or less Tabasco sauce (to suit your spicy threshold).

2. Pour into molds, leaving a little space at the top for them to expand. Insert sticks and freeze until hard (at least 8 hours). If mixture is too liquidy for sticks to stand straight up, let freeze for about 1 hour, then insert sticks.

3. Run the mold under warm water for a few seconds to loosen them up, then remove from the mold.

Calories 31   **Fat** 0 g   **Saturated Fat** 0 g   **Carbs** 2.7 g   **Fiber** 0.2 g   **Sugar** 1.9 g   **Alcohol** 3 g   **Protein** 0.4 g

Cappuccino

My ideal Saturday involves taking the train into Rotterdam to have a large cappuccino at my favorite café. The barista inevitably feels it necessary to point out just how big a "large" cappuccino is, at which point my stuttering attempt to speak Dutch gives away my American-ness, and then everything makes sense to them. Americans like everything bigger! What's a girl gotta do to get a giant cappuccino around here? I digress. Here are my favorite cappuccino ice pops.

difficulty  **Yields: about 2 cups, 8 (2-oz.) pops**

1 cup coffee, chilled
3 Tbsp honey or sugar, divided
1 cup canned coconut milk

1. Stir to combine coffee and 2 tablespoons honey. In a separate bowl, combine coconut milk and remaining tablespoon of honey.

2. Pour coffee mixture into mold so that each well is about half-filled. Gently pour coconut milk over coffee. For more defined layers, place an upside-down spoon just over the coffee layer, then trickle the coconut milk over the spoon so that it slowly pours onto the coffee layer, leaving some space at the top for them to expand. You can also just freeze the coffee layer first, but this creates two distinct layers and I like the frothy look of cappuccinos to show! Insert sticks and freeze until hard (at least 4 hours).

3. Run the mold under warm water for a few seconds to loosen them up, then remove from the mold.

Calories 93   **Fat** 7.2 g   **Saturated Fat** 6.3 g   **Carbs** 8.2 g   **Fiber** 0.7 g   **Sugar** 7.5 g   **Protein** 0.8 g

Caramel Macchiato

My love affair with iced coffee began with an obsession over ice caramel macchiatos in college (a star player in my Freshman 15). But that salted caramel goodness can be replicated in healthy, low glycemic index form with the help of dates! Naturally caramel-tasting and sweetened with slow-burning sugars, they add flavor and fiber to these macchiato pops.

difficulty 🍦🍦🍦   **Yields: about 2 cups, 8 (2-oz.) pops**

½ cup pitted Medjool dates (8–10)
1 cup coffee, chilled
Pinch of salt
¾ cup canned coconut milk
2 Tbsp honey
½ tsp vanilla extract

1. Soak dates in hot water for at least 30 minutes to soften. Drain water. Blend dates, coffee, and salt until smooth.

2. Pour into molds so that each is about half full, insert sticks, and freeze until hard (or at least 2 hours).

3. Stir to combine coconut milk, honey, and vanilla, then pour into the remaining space of each mold, leaving a little room at the top for them to expand. Return to the freezer until hard.

4. Run the mold under warm water for a few seconds to loosen them up, then remove from the mold.

Calories 117   **Fat** 7.2 g   **Saturated Fat** 6.3 g   **Carbs** 14.4 g   **Fiber** 1.6 g   **Sugar** 12.4 g   **Protein** 1 g

Carrot Cake

Which love came first: that for carrot cake or that for cream cheese frosting? It's hard to say, what with the two being irreplaceable elements of what experts have dubbed the best cake ever (just kidding, experts don't say that, it's me, I say that). Naturally, both elements had to be incorporated into this pop, with the top full of cream cheese frosting goodness and the bottom packed with carrots and spices.

difficulty   **Yields: about 2 cups, 8 (2-oz.) pops**

Cream cheese frosting layer
- ¼ cup cream cheese
- ¼ cup plain Greek yogurt
- 1 Tbsp honey

Carrot cake layer
- 2 carrots, roughly chopped (about ½ cup)
- 1 banana
- ½ cup plain Greek yogurt
- 2 Tbsp honey
- 1 tsp ground cinnamon
- ¼ tsp ground cloves

1. For the frosting layer, stir to combine cream cheese, yogurt, and honey. Spoon a dollop into the bottom of each well.

2. Combine carrots, banana, yogurt, honey, cinnamon, and cloves in a blender until smooth. Pour into molds, leaving a little space at the top for them to expand. Insert sticks and freeze until hard (at least 4 hours).

3. Run the mold under warm water for a few seconds to loosen them up, then remove from the mold.

Calories 90   **Fat** 3.9 g   **Saturated Fat** 2.5 g   **Carbs** 13.2 g   **Fiber** 0.9 g   **Sugar** 10.5 g   **Protein** 1.7 g

Cherry Limeade

Can we take a second to acknowledge how maraschino cherries nearly ruined us for real cherries? Because obviously 8-year-old me was all heart-eyed-emoji for these bleached, dyed, syrup-infused sugar bombs. So much so that when I first tasted real cherries, the letdown was serious. But once the fog of the sugar high is lifted, we come to realize that cherries don't need to be of the maraschino variety to taste really good (especially when cooked down with lime into deeply sweet, blissfully tart perfection).

difficulty   **Yields: about 2 cups, 8 (2-oz.) pops**

3 cups pitted cherries (fresh or frozen)
½ cup water
¼ cup honey or sugar
¼ cup lime juice (2 limes)
2 Tbsp finely grated lime zest (2 limes)

1. Add all ingredients to a small saucepan over medium/high heat and cook with the lid on until cherries have mostly burst and mixture is bubbling, about 10 minutes.

2. Slightly mash any remaining cherries and spoon into molds, leaving a little space at the top for them to expand. Insert sticks and freeze until hard (at least 4 hours).

3. Run the mold under warm water for a few seconds to loosen them up, then remove from the mold.

Calories 60   **Fat** 0 g   **Saturated Fat** 0 g   **Carbs** 15.5 g   **Fiber** 1.1 g   **Sugar** 13.7 g   **Protein** 0.5 g

Tip: Drop a few chocolate chips into your mold after you fill them with the almond mixture. If you notice they sink to the bottom, freeze the mixture first for an hour, then add the chips and insert the sticks, returning to the freezer until completely frozen.

Chocolate Chip Cookie Dough

My ideal chocolate chip cookie is baked just long enough that the dough melts into flat cookie-esque rounds. There should be minimal crispiness (and thus maximal raw cookie doughness). Some local cafés have hopped on board, serving ice cream cones filled high with scoops of pure cookie dough, but these are often laden with butter and sugar. So in the name of creating a popsicle reminiscent of everyone's favorite guilty pleasure (with a lot less of the guilt), we're turning to almonds to bring our cookie dough fantasies to life.

difficulty   **Yields: about 2 cups, 8 (2-oz.) pops**

1 cup milk (can substitute dairy-free)
½ cup finely ground almond flour
½ cup almond butter
2 Tbsp packed brown sugar (can substitute no-calorie sweetener)
1 tsp vanilla extract
Pinch of salt
¼ cup dark or milk chocolate chips

1. Combine all ingredients except chocolate chips in a blender until evenly mixed.

2. Pour into molds, leaving a little space at the top for them to expand. Sprinkle in chocolate chips (you can add more or less, depending on how chocolatey you want your pops). Insert sticks and freeze until hard (at least 4 hours).

3. Run the mold under warm water for a few seconds to loosen them up, then remove from the mold.

Calories 161   **Fat** 12.1 g   **Saturated Fat** 2.2 g   **Carbs** 10.3 g   **Fiber** 2 g   **Sugar** 7.1 g   **Protein** 5.2 g

Cookies and Cream

I consider myself an Oreo purist. It's Original/Double Stuffed or bust. But at almost 50 calories a cookie combined with my ability to reach an upwards of 4 cpm (cookies per minute), it's just not a sustainable snacking habit. These popsicles find a way to stretch that Oreo goodness out, lacing a lightened-up cream cheese and yogurt blend with crumbled Oreos. Throw a whole cookie into each popsicle well for an added treat.

difficulty 🍦🍦🍦   **Yields: about 2 cups, 8 (2-oz.) pops**

1½ cups vanilla yogurt
¼ cup cream cheese
¼ cup milk (can substitute dairy-free)
2 Tbsp honey or sugar (can substitute no-calorie sweetener)
1 tsp vanilla extract
¼ cup crushed Oreo cookies (about 4 cookies) + 1 whole cookie for each popsicle well (optional)

1. Whisk together all ingredients (except cookies) until smooth. Stir in crushed cookies.

2. Pour into molds, leaving a little space at the top for them to expand. Optionally, put a whole cookie into each mold for a hidden treat by filling the molds halfway, setting in a cookie, then topping off to fill each well. Tap firmly on the counter to remove bubbles. Insert sticks and freeze until hard (at least 4 hours).

3. Run the mold under warm water for a few seconds to loosen them up, then remove from the mold.

Nutrition information includes 4 crushed cookies, not the optional whole cookies.

Calories 106   **Fat** 6.3 g   **Saturated Fat** 3.6 g   **Carbs** 10 g   **Fiber** 0.2 g   **Sugar** 8.3 g   **Protein** 2.8 g

Tip: Not a fan of grapefruit? This recipe works well with just about any citrus fruit! You will likely need less honey or sugar with sweeter fruits (like oranges), so start with 2 Tbsp, taste the mixture, and add more as needed.

Creamy Pink Grapefruit

Did you know that each of the main tastes indicate something specific, dating back to caveman times of keeping us humans eating the right things? Sweetness points to energy-dense sugars, saltiness to electrolytes, sourness to acids, umami to proteins, and bitter? We taste bitter to identify natural toxins! This isn't to say everything bitter is poisonous, of course, but it explains why bitter things like coffee, beer, and grapefruit can be a love/hate thing for people. But with a bit of cream and sweetener, you can counteract the bitterness of grapefruit, bringing out its naturally bright and citrusy flavors!

difficulty   Yields: about 2 cups, 8 (2-oz.) pops

1½ cups grapefruit juice
¼ cup cream cheese
¼ cup honey or sugar
½ grapefruit, peeled and thinly sliced

1. Whisk together grapefruit juice, cream cheese, and honey until smooth.

2. Pour into molds about ¾ of the way full, then add a slice of grapefruit to each well. Insert sticks and freeze until hard (at least 4 hours).

3. Run the mold under warm water for a few seconds to loosen them up, then remove from the mold.

Calories 84   **Fat** 3.3 g   **Saturated Fat** 2 g   **Carbs** 13.5 g   **Fiber** 0.9 g   **Sugar** 12.7 g   **Protein** 1.6 g

Cucumber Spa

If there's one thing that makes European spas great (besides strategically planning your visit on a designated "bathing suit day"), it's the spa water served. This cucumber- and mint-infused amenity is perhaps even more refreshing than the bucket of ice cold water the spa-goers have a habit of dumping onto their heads after a sit in the sauna. So for the days when it's so hot that you want to dump a bucket of ice water on your head, these pops are the answer.

difficulty   **Yields: about 2 cups, 8 (2-oz.) pops**

1 cup water
¼ cup fresh lime juice (2 limes)
¼ cup honey or sugar
1 cup loosely packed mint (on the stem, if possible)
½ cucumber

1. Add water, lime juice, and honey to a small saucepan over medium heat. Heat until hot and steaming, but not boiling, then remove from heat and add mint leaves. Stir to combine and let mint leaves steep for 15 minutes, covered. Remove the mint and set aside to let mixture cool to lukewarm (quicken this up by setting the pan in a sink full of cold water).

2. Meanwhile, thinly slice the cucumber lengthwise into strips (using a vegetable peeler or mandoline slicer makes this easy). Alternatively, slice cucumber into thin rounds.

3. Evenly distribute the minty lime water into each mold, then add the sliced cucumber. Top off with water as needed to fill the molds nearly to the top. Insert sticks and freeze until hard (at least 4 hours).

4. Run the mold under warm water for a few seconds to loosen them up, then remove from the mold.

Calories 29   **Fat** 0.1 g   **Saturated Fat** 0 g   **Carbs** 7.9 g   **Fiber** 0.1 g   **Sugar** 6.8 g   **Protein** 0.2 g

Darling Lemon Thyme

As an American living abroad, I do what I can to bring the tastes of home to my kitchen (and let me tell ya, the weekly shipments of Chipotle burritos and ranch dressing are getting expensive). So I've had to learn to create some of my favorite comfort foods from scratch. I'm talking buttermilk biscuits and pancakes. But I always find myself with buttermilk leftover that goes to waste (there are people who can drink the stuff; I am not one of them). Had I known, however, that buttermilk is a key ingredient in what is quite possibly one of my favorite recipes in this book (I said it, folks), life would have been infinitely more delicious.

difficulty

Yields: about 2 cups, 8 (2-oz.) pops

½ cup fresh lemon juice (3 lemons)
½ cup honey or sugar
6 sprigs of thyme
2 Tbsp finely grated lemon zest (2 lemons)
1½ cups fresh buttermilk

1. Set a small saucepan over medium heat and add lemon juice, honey, thyme sprigs, and lemon zest. Cook for 3 to 5 minutes, stirring frequently, until sugar has dissolved. Fish out the sprigs of thyme; it's okay if a few pesky leaves remain. Let cool to lukewarm (quicken this up by setting the pan in a sink full of cold water).

2. Mix buttermilk into mixture and pour into molds, leaving a little space at the top for them to expand. Insert sticks and freeze until hard (at least 4 hours).

3. Run the mold under warm water for a few seconds to loosen them up, then remove from the mold.

Calories 72   **Fat** 0.6 g   **Saturated Fat** 0.4 g   **Carbs** 15.8 g   **Fiber** 0.4 g   **Sugar** 15.1 g   **Protein** 1.8 g

Dulce Date Leche

Anyone who knows me well can attest to my sweet tooth, which has a tendency to be the devil on my shoulder telling me, "That sugary cereal for dinner is a totally okay thing to do." That sugar devil unexpectedly hit her peak in Argentina, the land of steak and mate tea. Because in addition to their love of all things beef, Argentinians have a love affair with dulce de leche, a creamy dreamy caramel-like spread that I obviously worked into half of the meals I consumed while in the country. But with the naturally caramel sweetness of dates and creaminess of coconut, we can make healthier popsicles that take your tastes buds on the dulce de leche train straight to Buenos Aires!

difficulty **Yields: a little less than 2 cups, 6–8 (2-oz.) pops**

½ cup pitted Medjool dates (8–10)
1 (14-oz.) can coconut milk
¼ tsp vanilla extract
Pinch of salt

1. Soak dates in hot water for at least 30 minutes to soften. Drain water.

2. Combine all ingredients in a blender until smooth.

3. Pour into molds, leaving a little space at the top for them to expand. Insert sticks and freeze until hard (at least 4 hours).

4. Run the mold under warm water for a few seconds to loosen them up, then remove from the mold.

Calories 151   **Fat** 10.1 g   **Saturated Fat** 7 g   **Carbs** 13.6 g   **Fiber** 1 g   **Sugar** 10.1 g   **Protein** 1.3 g

Tip: For ultra-rich pops, replace half of the milk in this recipe with strong brewed coffee! Just be sure to chill the coffee beforehand.

Dutch Cookie Butter

Among the foods I gorged on in my first days of living in the Netherlands were cheese, stroopwafels, poffertjes, and stamppot. But rising above them all as the food I could, if necessary, live on? The speculoos butter! Speculoos is a spiced shortbread cookie that, when whipped into a creamy nut butter-like spread, is decidedly irresistible. But with a single tablespoon containing a hefty 90 calories, I began work on stripping this spreadable gold down to its basics, and found that the key is all in the spices! These pops ditch a lot of that sugar and butter, using almonds for their creaminess and a blend of spices for that distinct Dutch cookie flavor.

difficulty

Yields: a little less than 2 cups, 6–8 (2-oz.) pops

1 cup milk (can substitute dairy-free)
½ cup finely ground almond flour
½ cup almond butter
2–4 Tbsp packed brown sugar, to taste
2 tsp ground cinnamon
½ tsp nutmeg
½ tsp ground cloves
¼ tsp ground ginger
Pinch of ground white pepper
Pinch of salt

1. Combine all ingredients in a blender until evenly mixed, adding more or less brown sugar to suit your taste.

2. Pour into molds, leaving a little space at the top for them to expand. Insert sticks and freeze until hard (at least 4 hours).

3. Run the mold under warm water for a few seconds to loosen them up, then remove from the mold.

Calories 73 • **Fat** 4.8 g • **Saturated Fat** 0.7 g • **Carbs** 6.1 g • **Fiber** 1.2 g • **Sugar** 3.9 g • **Protein** 2.8 g

Eat Your Protein

I know this is just a book about the humble popsicle, but can we geek out on some nutrition science real quick? Because I want to tell you about the Protein Leverage Hypothesis (are your eyes glazing over yet?). This is a theory that basically says if you don't eat enough protein, you'll inadvertently eat more calories overall (more fat, carbs, protein . . . the works) until you get the protein your body needs. In short: not enough protein = eat more food than you need. So really, you're doing a service to yourself by blending up a batch of these more-protein-than-your-average-popsicles pops.

difficulty   **Yields: about 2 cups, 8 (2-oz.) pops**

1½ cups cottage cheese
1 heaping cup blueberries (fresh or frozen and thawed)
2–4 Tbsp honey, to taste
Splash of milk, as needed
Optional: 2 Tbsp chia seeds

1. Combine all ingredients in a blender until smooth, adding a splash of milk as needed to get things moving. You can add more or less honey to suit your taste, and can stir in chia seeds after blending for an added boost of protein and healthy fat.

2. Pour into molds, leaving a little space at the top for them to expand. Insert sticks and freeze until hard (at least 4 hours).

3. Run the mold under warm water for a few seconds to loosen them up, then remove from the mold.

Calories 79   **Fat** 1.6 g   **Saturated Fat** 0.5 g   **Carbs** 9.8 g   **Fiber** 1.7 g   **Sugar** 6.3 g   **Protein** 6.7 g

Tip: For distinct layers, freeze each portion completely before you pour in the next. If you have trouble getting your popsicle sticks to stand up when making the first layer, use aluminum foil to keep them upright. Simply cover your mold tightly with foil, then push the sticks through the foil and into each well, making sure that the stick is submerged in the red layer.

Firecracker

Fresh summer berries and creamy coconut milk make up these nostalgic pops (without all the high fructose corn syrup of said nostalgic pops). So go buy you and the crew your annual American flag shirts, dig up your jorts, and whip up a batch of these patriotic pops for your all-American 4th of July celebrations.

difficulty   **Yields: about 2 cups, 8 (2-oz.) pops**

Red
> 1 cup quartered strawberries (fresh or frozen and thawed)
> 1 Tbsp honey
> 1 Tbsp lemon juice (½ of a lemon)

White
> ⅔ cup canned coconut milk
> 1 Tbsp honey

Blue
> ⅔ cup blueberries (fresh or frozen and thawed)
> 2 Tbsp canned coconut milk
> 1 Tbsp honey
> Optional: blue food coloring or blue spirulina powder

1. Combine all "Red" ingredients in a blender until smooth. Pour evenly into the bottom of molds (you can use a small measuring cup to portion out even layers).

2. Cover the mold tightly with aluminum foil then push popsicle sticks through the foil into each well so that they stick in the red mixture. The aluminum will help to keep the sticks standing straight! Freeze until solid, at least 2 hours.

3. Combine "White" ingredients. Pour evenly on top of the red layer. Return to the freezer until solid.

4. Combine all "Blue" ingredients in a blender until smooth, optionally adding a few drops of food coloring or a dash of spirulina to enhance the blue color. Pour evenly on top of the white layer and return to the freezer until solid.

5. Run the mold under warm water for a few seconds to loosen them up, then remove from the mold.

Calories 89   **Fat** 5.5 g   **Saturated Fat** 4.8 g   **Carbs** 10.9 g   **Fiber** 1.2 g   **Sugar** 9.3 g   **Protein** 0.9 g

Frosé Sangria

An ideal summer shouldn't involve all that many hard decisions. But it does. Like how best to enjoy that perfectly sunny day, or which bathing suit to wear, or how many s'mores is too many s'mores. And if there's one thing that just should not be a decision, it's which boozy refreshment is going to cool you off. Which is why these Frosé Sangria pops are the best of both worlds: fruity sangria and frozen rosé!

difficulty   **Yields: about 2 cups, 8 (2-oz.) pops**

1 cup dry rosé wine
½ cup orange juice
2 Tbsp honey or sugar
½ heaping cup fresh fruit, such as: orange slices, diced mango, sliced strawberry

1. Whisk together wine, juice, and honey until evenly mixed.

2. Loosely set fruit into each popsicle well. Pour in the wine mixture, leaving a little space at the top for them to expand. Firmly tap on the counter to remove air pockets, then insert sticks and freeze until hard (at least 8 hours).

3. Run the mold under warm water for a few seconds to loosen them up, then remove from the mold.

Calories 70   **Fat** 0.1 g   **Saturated Fat** 0 g   **Carbs** 8.1 g   **Fiber** 0.2 g   **Sugar** 6.1 g   **Alcohol** 5.4 g   **Protein** 0.2 g

Tip: Which to use, Dutch process cocoa powder or natural? "Dutched" powder has been treated with an alkaline solution to neutralize the acidity, meaning it is less sharp and sour tasting than natural cocoa powder. While the distinction between the two can make or break baked goods, you can use either cocoa powder when making these pops.

Fudge

One of my greatest culinary revelations came when I realized cocoa powder isn't all that bad for you (and dare I say, healthy?). Made from the fibrous cocoa solids that are left after squeezing the cocoa butter out of the beans, cocoa powder is basically concentrated chocolate flavor (without all the sugar). And when combined with the frozen coconut milk and a drizzle of rich maple syrup, you get intensely chocolatey Fudge Pops that blow the classic store-bought variety out of the water.

difficulty

Yields: 1½ cups, 6 (2-oz.) pops

1 (14-oz.) can coconut milk
½ cup unsweetened cocoa powder
4–6 Tbsp maple syrup or honey, to taste
1 tsp vanilla extract
Pinch of salt

1. Whisk together all ingredients, adding more or less maple syrup to suit your taste.

2. Pour into molds, leaving a little space at the top for them to expand. Insert sticks and freeze until hard (at least 4 hours).

3. Run the mold under warm water for a few seconds to loosen them up, then remove from the mold.

Calories 205 **Fat** 16.8 g **Saturated Fat** 14.6 g **Carbs** 16.6 g **Fiber** 3.8 g **Sugar** 10.4 g **Protein** 2.9 g

Ginger Pear

If my relationship with ginger were a line graph, it would waver around zero for my whole life. Until college, that is, when I survived exclusively on what's-in-my-fridge stir fry, at which point the line graph goes steeply uphill. There's a little dip in the graph when I finally get sick of stir fry (and move on to a daily ritual of microwaved potatoes), but it then recovers and goes infinitely up when I learn how to pair ginger with, well, everything. Ginger brings a distinct zing to both savory and sweet recipes. You can put as little or as much as you want in these pops, just taste the mixture before freezing and adjust!

difficulty   **Yields: about 2 cups, 8 (2-oz.) pops**

    2 ripe pears
    1 cup water
    2 Tbsp honey
    1–2 Tbsp grated fresh ginger, to taste

1. Combine all ingredients in a blender until smooth. Start with 1 tablespoon of ginger, taste, and add more to suit your liking (keep in mind that the flavors will taste less strong when frozen).

2. Pour into molds, leaving a little space at the top for them to expand. Insert sticks and freeze until hard (at least 4 hours).

3. Run the mold under warm water for a few seconds to loosen them up, then remove from the mold.

Calories 40   **Fat** 0.1 g   **Saturated Fat** 0 g   **Carbs** 12.8 g   **Fiber** 1.7 g   **Sugar** 9.4 g   **Protein** 0.3 g

Tip: Have unripe pears? Stick them in a paper bag with a banana and scrunch it shut. Bananas give off a lot of ethylene gas, which is the compound responsible for ripening in many fruits. This will help the pears ripen faster!

Grape Sorbet

One of my most favorite summertime snacks is as simple as it is delicious—frozen grapes! When frozen then thawed for a few minutes, they're like miniature balls of grape sorbet. With a touch of lemon and sweetener, these ice pops are the leveled-up version!

difficulty

Yields: about 2 cups, 8 (2-oz.) pops

3 cups green grapes
2 Tbsp honey
1 tsp finely grated lemon zest (½ of a lemon)
1 tsp lemon juice (¼ of a lemon)

1. Combine all ingredients in a blender until smooth. Strain out skins by setting a wide bowl under a mesh sieve and pouring mixture through, using a rubber spatula to push out all the juice.

2. Pour into molds, leaving a little space at the top for them to expand. Insert sticks and freeze until hard (at least 4 hours).

3. Run the mold under warm water for a few seconds to loosen them up, then remove from the mold.

Calories 39   **Fat** 0.1 g   **Saturated Fat** 0.1 g   **Carbs** 10.3 g   **Fiber** 0.3 g   **Sugar** 9.9 g   **Protein** 0.3 g

Tip: *Are you the kinda person who likes pulp in their orange juice? If so, you probably won't need to strain the grape skins in the first step!*

Green Smoothie

There's something satisfying about packing in a serving of vegetables before 9:00 a.m. My go-to method for making it happen? Green smoothies. Naturally, a popsiclified version of my favorite green smoothie had to make it into this book. The recipe is flexible to whatever soon-to-go-bad fruits or greens you may have in your kitchen, and can be made fruity or creamy.

difficulty   **Yields: about 2 cups, 8 (2-oz.) pops**

1½ cups orange juice (you can substitute milk for a creamier pop)
1 cup spinach or kale
1 banana
1 kiwi (apples and pears work well too)
¼ cup honey
Optional: 1 Tbsp seeds (like chia or flax)

1. Combine all ingredients in a blender until smooth.

2. Pour into molds, leaving a little space at the top for them to expand. Insert sticks and freeze until hard (at least 4 hours).

3. Run the mold under warm water for a few seconds to loosen them up, then remove from the mold.

Calories 73   **Fat** 0.2 g   **Saturated Fat** 0 g   **Carbs** 18.5 g   **Fiber** 1 g   **Sugar** 15.3 g   **Protein** 0.7 g

Tip: *Unless you have a powerful blender, you can get pops that are ultra-smooth by blending the juice (or milk) and leafy greens together first, then adding in the rest of the ingredients. This helps to break down the greens to be ultra-fine (meaning no accidental spinach in your teeth!)*

Happy Birthday

I had a bit of a shock when I celebrated my first birthday living in the Netherlands. Birthdays growing up in America always meant being showered with cake and treats from friends and family. Like the cake my dad decorated for me on my 2nd birthday after having been the only man in his cake decorating class. Or my mom's infamously delicious cake made from a can of pumpkin puree and box of chocolate cake mix. But then I moved to the Netherlands, where it's customary for you to bring the cake to the party on your birthday. The nerve! But after a few laps around the sun, the tradition of bringing your own cake is beginning to grow on me, because you can pick the exact cake you want! And if that cake happens to be in the form of rainbow sprinkle–laced cake batter pops, so be it.

difficulty

Yields: about 2 cups, 8 (2-oz.) pops

½ cup pitted Medjool dates (8–10)
¾ cup milk (can substitute dairy-free)
½ cup plain Greek yogurt
½ cup oats (rolled or instant)
2 Tbsp almond butter
1 tsp vanilla extract
Pinch of salt
¼ cup rainbow sprinkles

1. Soak dates in hot water for at least 30 minutes to soften. Drain water.

2. Combine all ingredients except sprinkles in a blender until smooth. Stir in the sprinkles.

3. Pour into molds, leaving a little space at the top for them to expand. Top each well with more sprinkles. Insert sticks and freeze until hard (at least 4 hours).

4. Run the mold under warm water for a few seconds to loosen them up, then remove from the mold.

Calories 124   **Fat** 4 g   **Saturated Fat** 1.1 g   **Carbs** 20.7 g   **Fiber** 1.8 g   **Sugar** 13.8 g   **Protein** 3.1 g

Honey Mint

Growing up, tea was always reserved for sick days, meaning that over time I learned to associate tea with being sick (a.k.a. I hated the stuff). It wasn't until I discovered a little tea shop in Amsterdam that my mind was changed. Like a candy shop of tea flavors, they had buckets full of delicious smelling blends. And so began my tea addiction. But the simple classic that never gets old? Fresh mint and honey tea!

difficulty **Yields: about 2 cups, 8 (2-oz.) pops**

1¾ cups coconut water
2 Tbsp honey
½ cup mint leaves (on the stem, if possible) + a few fresh sprigs for decoration

1. Add coconut water to a small saucepan over medium heat. Heat until hot and steaming, but not boiling, then remove from heat and stir in honey and mint. Let mint steep until the mixture has cooled to lukewarm (quicken this up by setting the pan in a sink full of cold water). Fish out mint.

2. Add fresh mint sprigs to each popsicle well and pour in the coconut water mixture, leaving a little space at the top for them to expand. Insert sticks and freeze until hard (at least 4 hours). If mixture is too liquidy for sticks to stand straight up, let freeze for about 1 hour, then insert sticks.

3. Run the mold under warm water for a few seconds to loosen them up, then remove from the mold.

Calories 28 **Fat** 0.2 g **Saturated Fat** 0.1 g **Carbs** 6.8 g **Fiber** 1 g **Sugar** 5.7 g **Protein** 0 g

Horchata

My first encounter with the term "horchata" was at a gas station in Atlanta. To beat the summer heat while visiting my grandparents in the summer, it became a ritual to stop by our favorite gas station to buy giant neon-colored slushies. Being the creative burgeoning foodie that I was, I would blend the slushies into such flavors as "Diet Mountain Dew + cherry slushy + orange creamsicle" (I'm not saying I was necessarily a skilled foodie). On one such culinary gas station escapade, I happened upon the horchata-flavored slushy, a creamy combination of rice and cinnamon. Unsure of how to blend it with Mountain Dew or Diet Coke, I filled the whole cup with pure horchata slush. And that was when I realized the deliciousness of simplicity.

difficulty

Yields: about 2 cups, 8 (2-oz.) pops

1 cup milk (can substitute dairy-free)
½ cup water
½ cup rice
2 tsp ground cinnamon
½ cup vanilla yogurt
¼ cup honey

1. Add milk and water to a medium saucepan and heat over medium until hot and steaming, but not boiling. Remove from heat then add rice and cinnamon. Allow rice to soak, with a lid on, for an hour.

2. Transfer to a blender and blitz until the mixture is as smooth as possible. Set a wide bowl under a mesh sieve and pour mixture through, using a rubber spatula to push out all the liquid. Discard the rice. Mix the yogurt and honey into the liquid.

3. Pour into molds, leaving a little space at the top for them to expand. Insert sticks and freeze until hard (at least 4 hours).

4. Run the mold under warm water for a few seconds to loosen them up, then remove from the mold.

Calories 102   **Fat** 0.9 g   **Saturated Fat** 0.6 g   **Carbs** 21 g   **Fiber** 0.5 g   **Sugar** 11.2 g   **Protein** 2.7 g

Tip: Separate eggs when they're still cold, then cover the bowl of egg whites and let it sit on the counter until it's room temperature. This way they're easiest to separate and whip up the fastest!

Igloo Baked Alaska

These popsicles are inspired by summers spent in the land of the midnight sun, where campfire toasted marshmallows are as bountiful as fresh wild berries. Simple and delicious on their own, we're leveling up these blueberry pops with a healthy heap of fluffy meringue that we'll toast to perfection.

difficulty   Yields: about 2 cups, 8 (2-oz.) pops

2 heaping cups blueberries (fresh or frozen and thawed)
2–4 Tbsp honey, to taste
2 Tbsp lemon juice (1 lemon)
3 large eggs, whites only
¼ tsp cream of tartar
½ cup sugar

1. Combine the berries, honey, and lemon juice in a blender until smooth, adding more or less honey depending on your taste and the tartness of your berries.

2. Pour into molds, leaving a little space at the top. Insert sticks and freeze until hard (at least 4 hours).

3. Just before removing pops from the freezer, make your igloo topping. Add egg whites and cream of tartar to a clean bowl and begin to whip with a standing or hand mixer. When eggs start to become foamy, gradually add in sugar. Continue whipping to stiff peaks (when you remove the beaters from the bowl, the egg whites should stand straight up without folding over).

4. Run the popsicle mold under warm water for a few seconds to loosen them up, then remove from the mold. Spoon on the igloo coating.

5. Use a kitchen torch to lightly toast the meringue. Serve immediately or return pops to the freezer on a parchment paper-lined plate until ready to eat (best when served on the same day).

Calories 73   **Fat** 0.2 g   **Saturated Fat** 0 g   **Carbs** 17.3 g   **Fiber** 0.9 g   **Sugar** 15.4 g   **Protein** 1.7 g

Tip: *Make this recipe vegan by using aquafaba instead of the egg whites. Simply replace the eggs with the juice from one 15-oz. can of chickpeas, whipping until you get stiff peaks.*

Jelly Pops

If you're anything like me, you have a forgotten jar of jam in the back of your fridge. You bought it, envisioning sit-down breakfasts with warm toast or fresh croissants and you thought I will definitely use this jam. But there it sits, in the back of your fridge. You wonder if it's safe to eat. But you don't throw it away. (Out of guilt? Out of hope that you'll eventually put it to use? The jury's still out.) Well, it's time we give that jam the attention it deserves in the form of these stupid-easy yet surprisingly-addictive pops!

difficulty   **Yields: about 2 cups, 8 (2-oz.) pops**

1½ cups plain Greek yogurt
2 Tbsp honey
½ cup jelly, jam, or fruit preserves (any flavor)

1. In a small bowl, stir to combine yogurt and honey.

2. Spoon some yogurt into each mold, followed by a bit of jelly or jam, followed by more yogurt. Continue adding each, in alternating layers, until you've used it all. You can either stir the layers a bit to create swirls, or leave as is for more distinct layers. Just be sure to leave a little space at the top for them to expand. Insert sticks and freeze until hard (at least 4 hours).

3. Run the mold under warm water for a few seconds to loosen them up, then remove from the mold.

Calories 113   **Fat** 2.6 g   **Saturated Fat** 1.7 g   **Carbs** 20.9 g   **Fiber** 0.2 g   **Sugar** 16.8 g   **Protein** 1.8 g

Tip: *For added yum, chop up some fruit and stir it in with the yogurt!*

Tip: No key limes? No problem. While key limes have a strong aroma that differs a bit from regular limes, we're packing in some major lime flavor with both juice and zest. Use whichever you can get your hands on!

Key Lime Pie

My quintessential summertime includes: grilling up Mom's famous zucchini corn salad, getting Dorito-y fingers by the beach, and making Key Lime Pie. One of these was deemed worthy of pop-ification. Acidity from the juice and flavor from the rind, combined with the creaminess of banana and yogurt, replicate the taste and feel of classic Key Lime Pie. And when frozen into refreshing popsicle form? The new quintessential summer.

difficulty   **Yields: about 2 cups, 8 (2-oz.) pops**

1 banana
¾ cup plain Greek yogurt
½ cup cream cheese
¼ cup fresh lime juice (2 limes, key lime or regular)
¼ cup honey
2 Tbsp finely grated lime zest (2 limes)
½ tsp vanilla extract
Optional topping: ½ cup graham cracker crumbs

1. Combine all ingredients except graham cracker crumbs in a blender until smooth.

2. Pour into molds, leaving a little space at the top for them to expand. Insert sticks and freeze until hard (at least 4 hours).

3. Run the mold under warm water for a few seconds to loosen them up, then remove from the mold. Optionally sprinkle with a dash of graham cracker crumbs (they stick best once the pops are a little soft).

Calories 123   **Fat** 6.5 g   **Saturated Fat** 4.1 g   **Carbs** 15.9 g   **Fiber** 1 g   **Sugar** 12.3 g   **Protein** 2.3 g

Tip: You can use flavored or unflavored kombucha in this recipe! Most fruity flavors will work well, along with ginger and hibiscus.

Kombucha Berry

It used to require self-made bribes to get myself to the grocery store, the reward usually being my favorite bottle of chia seed kombucha. But then I fell into the deep end of food blogging and suddenly my habit of buying kombucha with each grocery store visit became an expensive one. So I gave homebrewing a try and within a few weeks had my very own SCOBY, the alien pancake responsible for churning out weekly batches of refreshingly bubbly 'buch. So for the kombucha lovers out there, this one's for you.

difficulty    **Yields: about 2 cups, 8 (2-oz.) pops**

1 heaping cup mixed berries (fresh or frozen and thawed)
1 cup kombucha
2–4 Tbsp honey, to taste

1. Combine all ingredients in a blender until smooth, adding more or less honey depending on your taste and the tartness of the berries you use.

2. Pour into molds, leaving a little space at the top for them to expand. Insert sticks and freeze until hard (at least 4 hours). These pops tend to separate a little, which you can prevent if you'd like by freezing them for 1 hour, stirring each well, *then* inserting sticks and freezing until hard.

3. Run the mold under warm water for a few seconds to loosen them up, then remove from the mold.

Calories 30   **Fat** 0.1 g   **Saturated Fat** 0 g   **Carbs** 7.3 g   **Fiber** 0.6 g   **Sugar** 5.8 g   **Protein** 0.1 g

Tip: Bright and tart lemon juice is the spotlight of this recipe, so be sure to use fresh juice (not the bottled stuff) to avoid chemical tasting off-flavors.

Lemonade Stand

I was always an entrepreneurial little kid, picking up pinecones from neighbors' yards for a pretty penny (as in, literally for a penny per pinecone) and selling cookies alongside our family's yearly yard sale. But one classic entrepreneurial endeavor I never tried? A lemonade stand! So if you'll indulge me, these Lemonade Stand Popsicles are the deliciously refreshing manifestation of my childhood saleswoman dreams.

difficulty   **Yields: about 2 cups, 8 (2-oz.) pops**

1½ cups water
½ cup fresh lemon juice (3 lemons)
¼ cup honey or sugar
1 Tbsp finely grated lemon zest (1 lemon)

1. Stir together all ingredients, mixing well to evenly combine with the honey.

2. Pour into molds, leaving a little space at the top for them to expand. Freeze for 1 hour (until slushy), then stir each mold to equally disperse the lemon zest. Insert sticks and freeze until hard (at least 4 hours).

3. Run the mold under warm water for a few seconds to loosen them up, then remove from the mold.

Calories 36   **Fat** 0.1 g   **Saturated Fat** 0.1 g   **Carbs** 9.2 g   **Fiber** 0.1 g   **Sugar** 9.1 g   **Protein** 0.2 g

Tip: You can make these Strawberry Lemonade Pops by reducing the water to 1¼ cups and adding a heaping ¼ cup of finely chopped strawberries. Just sprinkle the strawberries into each well and top with the lemonade mixture!

Liliko'i Mango

It took me an embarrassing amount of time after falling in love with all things liliko'i on Maui to realize it was simply the Hawaiian word for passion fruit. But whether you call it passion fruit, maracuya, granadilla, or liliko'i, I think we can all agree that a ripe passion fruit is quite possibly the best thing ever, right? Powerfully tart and tropical, we're balancing it out with the natural sweetness of mango in these tropic-inspired pops.

difficulty

Yields: about 2 cups, 8 (2-oz.) pops

1 heaping cup chopped mango
1 cup passion fruit juice
2 Tbsp honey
Optional: seeds from 1 passion fruit

1. Combine mango, juice, and honey in a blender until smooth.

2. Pour into molds, leaving a little space at the top for them to expand. Optionally top each well with a spoonful of passion fruit seeds. Insert sticks and freeze until hard (at least 4 hours).

3. Run the mold under warm water for a few seconds to loosen them up, then remove from the mold.

Calories 57   **Fat** 0.3 g   **Saturated Fat** 0 g   **Carbs** 14.3 g   **Fiber** 3.4 g   **Sugar** 10.4 g   **Protein** 0.8 g

Tip: You can make your own passion fruit juice by scooping the pulp from 1 or 2 passion fruits into a mesh sieve that you've set over a small bowl. Push the juice through the sieve with the back of a spoon, then discard the seeds and pulp. Add water to reach 1 cup of liquid. You may need to add more honey or sweetener to compensate for the tartness of the fresh passion fruit juice.

Tip: If you're not big into sweets, this recipe is also great without the honey. Combine the coconut milk, vanilla, and chia seeds, then taste to see if you want honey in yours.

Mango Chia

Chia seeds are wondrous little beasts. While packing in some serious omega-3 fats and fiber, they also absorb moisture, turning liquids into nearly instant puddings! They give these pops a delightfully fun texture that holds up well in the summer heat.

difficulty

Yields: about 2 cups, 8 (2-oz.) pops

½ cup + a few tablespoons canned coconut milk, divided
¼ cup honey
¼ tsp vanilla extract
¼ cup chia seeds
1 cup mangoes, peeled, seeded, and diced

1. Stir to combine ½ cup coconut milk, honey, and vanilla, then mix in the chia seeds. Let sit for 15 minutes, or until chia seeds begin to thicken the liquid.

2. Spoon a bit of the chia mixture into each mold, followed by some mango and more chia. Continue adding each, in alternating layers, until you've used it all. Top each well off with a drizzle of coconut milk to even out the top, leaving a little space for them to expand. Insert sticks and freeze until hard (at least 4 hours).

3. Run the mold under warm water for a few seconds to loosen them up, then remove from the mold.

Calories 111   **Fat** 6.3 g   **Saturated Fat** 3.8 g   **Carbs** 14.8 g   **Fiber** 2.9 g   **Sugar** 11.5 g   **Protein** 2.1 g

Margarita

My margarita consumption used to peak on Cinco de Mayo, only to drop off steeply for the rest of the summer. But after living in San Antonio for a hot second (a blistering, over 100-degree, can't-stop-sweating hot second), I learned to appreciate margaritas for what they truly are . . . a survival mechanism. A deliciously citrusy, salty, intoxicating survival mechanism to combat the summer heat.

difficulty   **Yields: about 2 cups, 8 (2-oz.) pops**

1 cup orange juice
½ cup silver tequila
½ cup lime juice (4 limes)
2–4 Tbsp honey or agave nectar, to taste
1 Tbsp finely grated lime zest (1 lime)
Optional: coarse sea salt

1. Stir together all ingredients except sea salt, mixing well to evenly combine with the honey. Add more or less honey to suit your taste.

2. Pour into molds, leaving a little space at the top for them to expand. Freeze for 1 hour then stir to redistribute any zest that may have sunk. Insert sticks and freeze until hard (at least 8 hours).

3. Run the mold under warm water *very briefly* to loosen them up, then remove from the mold. Optionally sprinkle with a pinch of sea salt.

Calories 72   **Fat** 0.1 g   **Saturated Fat** 0 g   **Carbs** 10.3 g   **Fiber** 1 g   **Sugar** 7.4 g   **Alcohol** 5.7 g   **Protein** 0.4 g

Tip: To make these pops alcohol-free, substitute ½ cup orange juice for the tequila.

Marshmallow Coconut Creme

We all know the noxiously sweet and sticky marshmallow spread of childhood, right? But do you know aquafaba? For the unfamiliar, aquafaba is the liquid that's in your can of chickpeas. Laced with starches and magic, it can be whipped up into glorious white, fluffy peaks. It's basically vegan egg white. And when frozen, the result is a light and airy pop that leaves you wondering how you're going to use all those leftover chickpeas this summer.

difficulty  **Yields: about 2 cups, 8 (2-oz.) pops**

½ cup aquafaba (the liquid from a 15-oz. can of chickpeas; liquid from home-cooked chickpeas will not work as well)
¼ tsp cream of tartar
¼ cup sugar
½ cup canned coconut milk
¼ tsp vanilla extract

1. Add chickpea liquid and cream of tartar to a clean bowl and begin to whip with a standing or hand mixer. When liquid starts to become foamy, gradually add in sugar. Continue whipping at high speed until you reach stiff peaks (when you remove the beaters from the bowl, the fluff should stand straight up without folding over). This can take a few minutes. Be patient, you'll get there. With beaters on, slowly pour in the coconut milk until fully incorporated. It will lose some fluff and become a bit liquid again; that's okay! Stir in vanilla.

2. Spoon or pour into molds, leaving a little space at the top for them to expand. Insert sticks and freeze until hard (at least 4 hours).

3. Run the mold under warm water for a few seconds to loosen them up, then remove from the mold.

Calories 61 **Fat** 3.6 g **Saturated Fat** 3.2 g **Carbs** 7.6 g **Fiber** 0.3 g **Sugar** 7.0 g **Protein** 0.5 g

Tip: Fruity cereals like Froot Loops and Fruity Pebbles work well in this recipe, but you can also go for chocolate with Cocoa Puffs or for more subtle flavors like corn flakes!

Milk and Cereal

Some flavor combinations are so commonplace that we don't stop to realize how great they are. That's right, people, I'm talking the cereal milk. You know, the milk that's left in the bowl after a big helping of breakfast cereal. But then Christina Tosi, culinary mastermind behind Momofuku Milk Bar bakery, came along and opened our eyes to the world of possibilities in what used to be a breakfast afterthought. We're using the same principles (and your favorite breakfast cereal) to whip up these nostalgic pops!

difficulty 🍦🍦🍦   **Yields: about 2 cups, 8 (2-oz.) pops**

2 cups of your favorite breakfast cereal, divided
1½ cups milk
½ cup vanilla yogurt
2 Tbsp maple syrup or packed brown sugar

1. Evenly divide ½ cup of the breakfast cereal into the bottom of each popsicle well, then place in the freezer to chill. Meanwhile, add milk and remaining 1½ cups of cereal to a medium bowl and stir. Let sit for 15 minutes, or until cereal softens and milk tastes strongly of cereal.

2. Set a wide bowl under a mesh sieve and pour in the cereal mixture, using a rubber spatula to push out the liquid while keeping the soggy cereal fibers in the sieve. Discard what's left in the sieve. Stir yogurt and maple syrup into the milk that collected in the bowl.

3. Remove mold with the dry cereal from the freezer and pour milk mixture into each well, leaving a little space at the top for them to expand. Tap firmly on the counter to remove any bubbles. Insert sticks and freeze until hard (at least 4 hours).

4. Run the mold under warm water for a few seconds to loosen them up, then remove from the mold.

Calories 75   **Fat** 1.4 g   **Saturated Fat** 0.8 g   **Carbs** 13 g   **Fiber** 0.8 g   **Sugar** 8.7 g   **Protein** 2.6 g

Mint Chocolate

My hobbies include thinking about food, eating food, and scheming up ways to trick unsuspecting friends and family into eating sneakily healthy food. And these mint pops? They definitely have a sneaky secret agenda. A heaping handful of fresh spinach adds a boost of nutrients while giving a pop of green to enhance the refreshing flavor of mint!

difficulty 🍦🍦🍦   **Yields: 1½ cups, 6 (2-oz.) pops**

1 (14-oz.) can coconut milk
¼ cup honey or sugar
1 cup loosely packed fresh mint leaves (on the stem, if possible)
1 cup fresh spinach
½ cup dark or milk chocolate (chips or a roughly chopped bar)

1. Add coconut milk and honey to a medium saucepan over medium-low heat. Heat until hot and steaming, but not boiling, stirring occasionally. Remove from heat and add mint leaves. Stir to combine and let mint leaves steep for 15 to 30 minutes. Fish out the mint and discard.

2. Add minty coconut milk and spinach to a blender. Puree until spinach is completely broken down.

3. Pour into molds, leaving a little space at the top for them to expand. Insert sticks and freeze until hard (at least 4 hours).

4. Just before removing pops from the freezer, add chocolate to a heat-resistant bowl. Bring a pot of water to a boil and set the bowl of chocolate over the boiling water (just above the water, not submerged). Stir constantly until most of the chocolate is melted. Remove the bowl from over the steam and continue to stir until chocolate has all melted.

5. Remove pops from the freezer and run the mold under warm water for a few seconds to loosen them up. Remove each popsicle from the mold, drizzle with chocolate, and (if you like) sprinkle with a dash of finely chopped chocolate.

Calories 219   **Fat** 13.5 g   **Saturated Fat** 9.4 g   **Carbs** 21.8 g   **Fiber** 1.6 g   **Sugar** 17.4 g   **Protein** 2.6 g

Mojito

I haven't encountered many responsible ways of drinking rum (looking at you, Jamaica 2012). But if ever there were a classy, cultivated means for consuming the stuff, it would be in these mojito pops. Because you're forced to take it slow, enjoying the hints of mint, lime, and rum all frozen together into thirst-quenching yet boozy (and above all, sophisticated) popsicles.

difficulty

Yields: about 2 cups, 8 (2-oz.) pops

1¼ cups water
¼ cup honey
¼ cup white rum
¼ cup fresh lime juice (2 limes)
1 Tbsp finely grated lime zest (1 lime)
½ cup mint on the stem

1. Whisk together water, honey, rum, lime juice, and lime zest in a cup until evenly mixed. Add sprigs of mint and gently muddle (using either a muddler or the handle of a wooden spoon) to release the mint oils. Mint should still be intact, not broken into pieces. Fish out the mint leaves.

2. Pour the mixture into molds, leaving a little space at the top for them to expand. Optionally add a few of the mint leaves to each mold for decoration. Freeze for 1 hour then stir to redistribute any zest that may have sunk. Insert sticks and freeze until hard (at least 8 hours).

3. Run the mold under warm water briefly to loosen them up, then remove from the mold.

Calories 54 **Fat** 0 g **Saturated Fat** 0 g **Carbs** 10.7 g **Fiber** 0.6 g **Sugar** 9 g **Alcohol** 2.3 g **Protein** 0.2 g

Mudslide

Mudslides were the original freakshake. Before we were adorning our unicorn-colored milkshakes with glazed donuts and cotton candy, the craziest thing we did to them was spike 'em with booze. Because nothing says "I'm on vacation" like vodka in your milkshake. But while the original mudslide packs a boozy punch with the addition of vodka, we're keeping it to coffee liqueur and Irish cream to allow these pops to freeze solid while keeping that decadent flavor.

difficulty   **Yields: about 2 cups, 8 (2-oz.) pops**

¼ cup coffee liqueur (like Kahlua)
¼ cup Irish cream (like Baileys)
½ cup coffee, chilled
1 cup canned coconut milk
¼ cup unsweetened cocoa powder
2–4 Tbsp honey or sugar, to taste

1. Whisk together all ingredients until smooth, adding more or less honey to suit your taste.

2. Pour into molds, leaving a little space at the top for them to expand. Insert sticks and freeze until hard (at least 8 hours). If mixture is too liquidy for sticks to stand straight up, let freeze for about 1 hour, then insert sticks.

3. Run the mold under warm water for a few seconds to loosen them up, then remove from the mold.

Calories 142   **Fat** 8.6 g   **Saturated Fat** 7.2 g   **Carbs** 12.1 g   **Fiber** 1.6 g   **Sugar** 6.7 g   **Alcohol** 3.2 g   **Protein** 1.5 g

Tip: If you tend to like your pops sweeter, blend an additional 1 Tbsp of honey into each layer.

Neapolitan Nice Cream

A trifecta of flavors for the person who can never seem to decide. Classic strawberry, vanilla, and chocolate take on a healthy twist in "nice cream" form. For the uninitiated, "nice cream" usually entails blending up some frozen bananas with a dash of milk into creamy, lower-calorie deliciousness. We're taking the concept a step further into these classic, healthified ice pops!

difficulty   **Yields: about 2 cups, 8 (2-oz.) pops**

Strawberry: ½ banana + ½ cup milk* + ½ cup quartered strawberries + 1 Tbsp honey
Vanilla: ½ banana + ½ cup milk* + 1 Tbsp honey + ½ tsp vanilla extract
Chocolate: ½ banana + ½ cup milk* + 1 Tbsp unsweetened cocoa powder

*can substitute dairy-free milk

1. Combine all of the strawberry layer ingredients in a blender until smooth. Pour into molds about ⅓ of the way full, trying not to spill the mixture on the sides of the molds. Firmly tap on the counter to remove the bubbles, insert sticks, and freeze until hard (at least 2 hours).

2. Combine all of the vanilla layer ingredients in a blender until smooth. Pour over the frozen strawberry layer about ⅔ of the way full, tap on the counter, and return to the freezer until hard (at least 2 hours).

3. Finally, combine all of the chocolate layer ingredients in a blender until smooth. Pour over the vanilla layer, leaving a little space at the top. Freeze until solid (at least 2 hours).

4. Run the mold under warm water for a few seconds to loosen them up, then remove from the mold.

Calories 64   **Fat** 1.1 g   **Saturated Fat** 0.6 g   **Carbs** 12.7 g   **Fiber** 1 g   **Sugar** 9.6 g   **Protein** 1.9 g

Tip: Use the aluminum foil trick to help your popsicle sticks stand upright when freezing the first layer. Cover your mold tightly with foil, then push the sticks through the foil and into each well, making sure the stick is submerged in the strawberry layer.

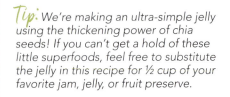

Tip: We're making an ultra-simple jelly using the thickening power of chia seeds! If you can't get a hold of these little superfoods, feel free to substitute the jelly in this recipe for ½ cup of your favorite jam, jelly, or fruit preserve.

Nut Butter and Jelly

Allergies are a weird thing, because they condition you to despise not only the allergen culprit (for me that's peanuts), but also its friends (i.e. all the nuts). So, I went through most of my life thinking all nuts were evil incarnated. But then I tasted almond butter for the first time and I entered into a new dimension of food love. Suddenly the jar of almond butter in my pantry was beckoning me (and a spoon) at all hours. I've since learned to tame the beast that is my almond butter infatuation, and channel it into more sensible methods of eating it . . . like NB&J!

difficulty   **Yields: about 2 cups, 8 (2-oz.) pops**

Jelly
  1 cup of your favorite berries (fresh or frozen)
  ½ tsp lemon juice
  2 Tbsp chia seeds
  Honey as needed

Nut Butter Base
  1 (14-oz.) can coconut milk
  ¼ cup of your favorite nut butter
  2 Tbsp honey
  Healthy pinch of salt

1. Add berries and lemon juice to a small saucepan and set over medium heat. Cook for 10 minutes, or until berries have burst and softened. Remove from heat and stir in chia seeds, mashing the fruit into a chunky jelly consistency. Taste and add honey as needed, 1 teaspoon at a time (it will depend on the sweetness of your berries). Set aside for 5 minutes to thicken.

2. Meanwhile, whisk together coconut milk, nut butter, honey, and salt.

3. Assemble pops by pouring a little of the nut butter mixture into each mold, followed by a spoonful of chia jelly. Continue adding the nut butter mixture and jelly, in alternating layers, until the molds are full. Insert sticks and freeze until hard (at least 4 hours).

4. Run the mold under warm water for a few seconds to loosen them up, then remove from the mold.

Calories 148   **Fat** 12.2 g   **Saturated Fat** 9.7 g   **Carbs** 10.2 g   **Fiber** 3.2 g   **Sugar** 6.7 g   **Protein** 2 g

Nutella Green Smoothie

Life is all about balance. Not enough water? Bad for you. Too much water? Also bad for you. It's about finding that sweet spot, which isn't a problem with these pops. You've got your spinach (filled with vitamins) balancing out your Nutella (filled with happiness). Like the yin and yang you never knew you needed.

difficulty   **Yields: about 2 cups, 8 (2-oz.) pops**

2 cups packed fresh spinach
1 cup milk (can substitute dairy-free)
2 bananas
½ cup Nutella

1. Combine all ingredients in a blender until smooth.

2. Pour into molds, leaving a little space at the top for them to expand. Insert sticks and freeze until hard (at least 4 hours).

3. Run the mold under warm water for a few seconds to loosen them up, then remove from the mold.

Calories 143   **Fat** 6.3 g   **Saturated Fat** 5.7 g   **Carbs** 20 g   **Fiber** 1.9 g   **Sugar** 15 g   **Protein** 2.5 g

Oatmeal Cookie

Oatmeal cookies must have identity issues. Everyone thinks they're chocolate chip cookies, only to be let down when the first bite reveals raisins and oats rather than chocolate and happiness. Well let's add fuel to the identity crisis fire, shall we? Because we're turning these classic second-favorite cookies into popsicles!

difficulty   **Yields: about 2 cups, 8 (2-oz.) pops**

1 banana
1 cup milk (can substitute dairy-free)
¼ cup oats (rolled or instant)
2 Tbsp honey or maple syrup
½ tsp vanilla extract
½ tsp ground cinnamon
¼ tsp ground ginger
Pinch of salt
½ cup raisins

1. Combine all ingredients except the raisins in a blender until smooth. Stir in the raisins.

2. Pour into molds, leaving a little space at the top for them to expand. Insert sticks and freeze until hard (at least 4 hours). If raisins sink to the bottom of the molds when you pour in the mix, let pops freeze for an hour, stir to move raisins back up, and return to the freezer until frozen solid.

3. Run the mold under warm water for a few seconds to loosen them up, then remove from the mold.

Calories 82   **Fat** 0.9 g   **Saturated Fat** 0.4 g   **Carbs** 18.3 g   **Fiber** 1.1 g   **Sugar** 12.9 g   **Protein** 1.8 g

Tip: *Rolled, instant, old-fashioned, steel-cut—so many oat varieties to choose from! Steel-cut oats are too chunky for this recipe. Rolled (a.k.a. old-fashioned) and instant oats, on the other hand, have been steamed and rolled to be more absorbent, so they're great for making these pops.*

Tip: Not a fan of bananas? Substitute the banana in this recipe for ¼ cup canned coconut milk and use a touch more honey than is called for.

Orange Creamsicles

Obviously in an encyclopedia of popsicles we have to include the classics, and is there any pop so nostalgic as the Orange Creamsicle? Juicy frozen orange surrounds a rich vanilla ice cream filling in the traditional version, but we're changing it up in the name of health and simplicity (but don't think for one second that we're compromising on flavor!).

difficulty   **Yields: about 2 cups, 8 (2-oz.) pops**

1 cup orange juice
1 banana
½ cup plain Greek yogurt
2 Tbsp honey
1 tsp vanilla extract
1 tsp orange zest (½ of an orange)

1. Combine all ingredients in a blender until smooth.

2. Pour into molds, leaving a little space at the top for them to expand. Insert sticks and freeze until hard (at least 4 hours). If mixture is too liquidy for sticks to stand straight up, let freeze for about 1 hour, then insert sticks.

3. Run the mold under warm water for a few seconds to loosen them up, then remove from the mold.

Calories 59 **Fat** 1 g **Saturated Fat** 0.6 g **Carbs** 12 g **Fiber** 0.5 g **Sugar** 9.7 g **Protein** 1 g

Orange Sunrise

My personality is such that I'm much more likely to go to bed at 4:00 a.m. than to wake up at such an unthinkable hour. But for some reason, I thought it was a good idea to join the rowing team for a hot second in college. The team who meets at 4:15 a.m. to drive an hour to a cold lake to row a boat. The team who wades into muddy water, boat over their heads, before the sun has even come up. And the team who is rewarded after a morning of working out with a breathtaking sunrise over a lake. Anyways, these pops replicate that early morning sunrise feeling (without all the, you know, waking up early stuff).

difficulty

Yields: about 2 cups, 8 (2-oz.) pops

1 cup chopped mango (fresh or frozen and thawed)
½ cup orange juice, divided
2 Tbsp honey, divided
1 cup quartered strawberries (fresh or frozen and thawed)

1. Blend mango, ¼ cup orange juice, and 1 tablespoon honey until smooth. Pour into the bottom half of your molds and rinse out the blender. Blend strawberries, remaining tablespoon of honey, and remaining ¼ cup orange juice. Pour to top off each mold, leaving a little space at the top for them to expand.

2. Use a popsicle stick or spoon to gently push the red layer into the orange to create swirls. Insert sticks and freeze until hard (at least 4 hours).

3. Run the mold under warm water for a few seconds to loosen them up, then remove from the mold.

Calories 41   **Fat** 0.2 g   **Saturated Fat** 0 g   **Carbs** 10.4 g   **Fiber** 0.7 g   **Sugar** 9.3 g   **Protein** 0.4 g

Paletas with Spiced Mango

Paletas are Mexican-style ice pops that tend to use an array of colorful fresh fruit, often combining them with unexpected spices. In the case of these ice pops, sweet mango is the main character while spicy chili and cayenne pepper play the supporting roles, adding complexity and kick.

difficulty   **Yields: about 2 cups, 8 (2-oz.) pops**

3 cups chopped mango (fresh or frozen and thawed)
2 Tbsp honey or agave nectar
2 Tbsp lime juice (1 lime)
¼ tsp chili powder
¼ tsp cayenne pepper
Pinch of salt

1. Finely chop 1 cup of the mango. Add the other 2 cups of mango to a blender with the other ingredients and blend until smooth. Stir in the chopped mango.

2. Pour into molds, leaving a little space at the top for them to expand. Insert sticks and freeze until hard (at least 4 hours).

3. Run the mold under warm water for a few seconds to loosen them up, then remove from the mold.

Calories 55   **Fat** 0.3 g   **Saturated Fat** 0.1 g   **Carbs** 14.1 g   **Fiber** 1.1 g   **Sugar** 12.9 g   **Protein** 0.6 g

Piña Colada

For many of us, piña coladas are the gateway cocktail. It's your first time trying alcohol, and between Mike's Hard Lemonade and that piña colada you had on vacation, you're thinking you could get used to this whole alcohol thing. As it turns out, some of us (oh heyyy) never learn to tolerate any other boozy beverages, and therefore any cocktail that successfully masks the alcohol within it is a good one. For my friends who know what I'm talking about (or for anyone looking to get transported to a beach in poptail form), these piña colada pops are calling you.

difficulty  **Yields: about 2 cups, 8 (2-oz.) pops**

1 heaping cup chopped pineapple
¾ cup canned coconut milk
¼ cup coconut rum (like Malibu)
2 Tbsp honey or sugar

1. Blitz all ingredients in a blender until smooth.

2. Pour into molds, leaving a little space at the top for them to expand. Insert sticks and freeze until hard (at least 8 hours).

3. Run the mold under warm water for a few seconds to loosen them up, then remove from the mold.

Calories 93   **Fat** 5.4 g   **Saturated Fat** 4.8 g   **Carbs** 9.9 g   **Fiber** 0.8 g   **Sugar** 8.7 g   **Alcohol** 1.2 g   **Protein** 0.7 g

Tip: Make these boozy pops alcohol-free by simple subbing the coconut rum for more coconut milk.

Pineapple Basil

My compulsion to not let food go to waste often ends in me throwing seemingly mismatched ingredients together in a smoothie or ice pop in a last-ditch effort to save them from eminent moldy doom. This has been known to result in some pretty weird flavor combos, but also some awesome ones. Case in point: pineapple + basil. It's a double whammy of flavors that shouldn't work together, but they do. They really, really do.

difficulty **Yields: about 2 cups, 8 (2-oz.) pops**

1½ cups chopped pineapple
½ cup coconut water
¼ cup loosely packed fresh basil leaves (dried basil will *not* work in this recipe)
2–4 Tbsp honey, to taste

1. Combine all ingredients in a blender until smooth, adding more or less honey to suit your taste.

2. Pour into molds, leaving a little space at the top for them to expand. Insert sticks and freeze until hard (at least 4 hours).

3. Run the mold under warm water for a few seconds to loosen them up, then remove from the mold.

Calories 34   **Fat** 0 g   **Saturated Fat** 0 g   **Carbs** 8.4 g   **Fiber** 0.4 g   **Sugar** 7.9 g   **Protein** 0.2 g

Tip: You can tell if your pineapple is ripe by either smelling the bottom (it should smell very sweet) or by trying to pluck a leaf from the center of the top (if the leaf comes out easily, it's ripe!).

Pineapple Coconut

Spending the winters of my childhood in Alaska required that we fly somewhere warm to thaw our bones come spring. Hawaii, a short(ish) plane ride away, was the usual destination. And on such bone-thawing retreats, I would inevitably eat so much sweet Hawaiian pineapple on the first day that my tongue stung from the bromelain overdose for the rest of the vacation. These pops? They solve that problem, slowing down your rate of pph (pineapples per hour) while still packing in the flavor of the tropics (and with just 3 ingredients!)

difficulty   **Yields: about 2 cups, 8 (2-oz.) pops**

1 cup coconut water
1 cup chopped pineapple
¼ cup honey

1. Blitz all ingredients in a blender until pineapple is roughly broken down. (Alternatively, use crushed pineapple instead of chopped pineapple, and simply stir everything together well.)
2. Pour into molds, leaving a little space at the top for them to expand. Insert sticks and freeze until hard (at least 4 hours).
3. Run the mold under warm water for a few seconds to loosen them up, then remove from the mold.

Calories 48   **Fat** 0.1 g   **Saturated Fat** 0.1 g   **Carbs** 12.6 g   **Fiber** 0.6 g   **Sugar** 11.5 g   **Protein** 0.4 g

Tip: Looking to save some time? You can often buy beets pre-roasted at the grocery store, which will cut some time out of this recipe (meaning less time between now and popsicles o'clock).

Pink Power Beet

Hands in the air if you think beets taste like dirt? No worries, I think the same! Which is why my main goal whenever I cook with beets is to make them . . . not taste like dirt. There are a few tricks to making this work, including roasting them to bring out their natural sweetness and combining them with creamy ingredients to cut through that sharp, earthy flavor.

difficulty

Yields: a bit over 2 cups, 8 (2-oz.) pops

1 medium red beet
1 Tbsp water
1 cup quartered strawberries (fresh or frozen and thawed)
¾ cup strawberry yogurt
¼ cup milk (can substitute dairy-free)
¼ cup honey

1. Preheat oven to 375° F. Trim, peel, and chop beet into half-inch cubes. Drizzle with 1 tablespoon water and place in an aluminum foil pouch. Bake for 50 minutes, or until fork-tender. Unwrap aluminum pouch and allow the beet to cool for 20 minutes.

2. Combine all ingredients in a blender until smooth.

3. Pour into molds, leaving a little space at the top for them to expand. Insert sticks and freeze until hard (at least 4 hours).

4. Run the mold under warm water for a few seconds to loosen them up, then remove from the mold.

Calories 70   **Fat** 0.5 g   **Saturated Fat** 0.3 g   **Carbs** 16 g   **Fiber** 0.6 g   **Sugar** 15.2 g   **Protein** 1.5 g

POG Juice

If you've ever visited Hawaii, there's a good chance you tried (and fell in love) with POG. What is POG, you ask? It's a tropical elixir made from the juices of passion fruit, orange, and guava. Served on the plane to the islands, served for breakfast every morning, and now served all summer long in popsicle form.

difficulty

Yields: about 2 cups, 8 (2-oz.) pops

½ cup finely chopped pineapple
⅔ cup passion fruit juice
⅔ cup orange juice
⅔ cup guava nectar
2 Tbsp honey

1. Evenly distribute the chopped pineapple into the bottom of each well.

2. Stir together the passion fruit, orange, and guava juices, along with the honey. Pour into molds, leaving a little space at the top for them to expand. Tap firmly on the counter to remove air pockets. Insert sticks and freeze until hard (at least 4 hours). If you want the pineapple pieces to be dispersed throughout the pop (and not just in the bottom), freeze for 1 hour, stir each well to move pineapple up, then insert the sticks and continue freezing until hard.

3. Run the mold under warm water for a few seconds to loosen them up, then remove from the mold.

Calories 55   **Fat** 0.1 g   **Saturated Fat** 0 g   **Carbs** 14.1 g   **Fiber** 0.2 g   **Sugar** 13.2 g   **Protein** 0.3 g

Tip: You should be able to find kefir in the refrigerated aisle near the yogurts; otherwise you can simply substitute for it with plain Greek yogurt.

Probiotic Mango Lassi

After falling in love with brewing kombucha, I decided to give homemade kefir a go. So I scoured the Dutch version of Craigslist for someone selling kefir grains (the starter) and biked across town to pick up what would become my kefir baby. She smelled faintly of SpaghettiOs when I first met her, so I tossed out the first few batches while she got used to her new home. But then one day I woke up and overnight she had created the most delicious, thick, creamy batch of kefir. Since then she's been churning out more kefir than I know what to do with, so naturally a popsicle was bound to emerge.

difficulty   **Yields: about 2 cups, 8 (2-oz.) pops**

1¼ cups milk kefir (can substitute plain Greek yogurt)
1 heaping cup chopped mango (fresh or frozen and thawed)
2–4 Tbsp honey or sugar, to taste

1. Combine all ingredients in a blender until smooth, adding more or less honey to suit your taste.

2. Pour into molds, leaving a little space at the top for them to expand. Insert sticks and freeze until hard (at least 4 hours).

3. Run the mold under warm water for a few seconds to loosen them up, then remove from the mold.

Calories 47   **Fat** 0.8 g   **Saturated Fat** 0.5 g   **Carbs** 9.3 g   **Fiber** 0.7 g   **Sugar** 8.7 g   **Protein** 1.2 g

Pupsicles

For when the puppers is being *such a good boyyy, yes you aaarrre*, they deserve a treat of epic proportions. These Pupsicles will do the trick, making for a happy, healthy, cooled-down doggo. Use silicone paw-shaped molds to make pops like in the picture, or use your standard popsicle mold with edible sticks, like carrots or dog treats!

difficulty   **Yields: a little less than 2 cups, 6–8 (2-oz.) pops**

1 cup low-fat or fat-free plain yogurt
1 banana
½ cup peanut butter
Dash of water to get things moving
Edible stick ideas: dog treats, carrot sticks, or celery

1. Combine all ingredients in a blender until smooth.

2. Pour into molds, leaving a little space at the top for them to expand. Depending on the shape of your pupsicle mold, you may insert an edible stick (such as dog treats, carrots, or celery). Freeze until hard (at least 4 hours).

3. Run the mold under warm water for a few seconds to loosen them up, then remove from the mold.

Calories 135   **Fat** 9.9 g   **Saturated Fat** 2.9 g   **Carbs** 8.4 g   **Fiber** 1.3 g   **Sugar** 5.2 g   **Protein** 5.3 g

Tip: *Be sure to use a low-fat yogurt that doesn't contain any artificial sweeteners. Excess fat can be hard on their pancreas, and artificial sweeteners (such as Xylitol) can be toxic.*

Tip: These also make for colorfully refreshing ice cubes! Just chop the fruit a bit more finely and freeze in a standard ice cube tray.

Rainbow Fruit

If having a sweet tooth is hereditary, mine was surely passed down from my grandfather. With him living in the south and loving dessert, you'd think the popsicle inspired by him would be something of the Sweet Potato Pie nature. But alas, his go-to ice pop for beating the Georgia heat is the simple combination of fresh fruit and coconut water. Keeping to my grandfather's method of cooking, the recipe is completely flexible. You can use whatever fruits are in season in your area and sweeten the pops to your liking!

difficulty   **Yields: about 2 cups, 8 (2-oz.) pops**

1 cup assorted fresh fruit, such as:
    ¼ cup sliced strawberries
    ¼ cup sliced kiwi
    ¼ cup blueberries
    ¼ cup chopped mango
1–1½ cups coconut water
2–4 Tbsp honey or agave nectar, to taste

1. Evenly distribute the fruit into molds, making sure not to pack them too tightly so the coconut water can fill the gaps.

2. Whisk together coconut water and honey, adding more or less honey to suit your taste. Pour over fruit, leaving a little space at the top for them to expand. Gently tap the pop mold on the counter to remove air pockets. Insert sticks and freeze until hard (at least 4 hours).

3. Run the mold under warm water for a few seconds to loosen them up, then remove from the mold.

Calories 16   **Fat** 0.1 g   **Saturated Fat** 0.1 g   **Carbs** 3.7 g   **Fiber** 0.8 g   **Sugar** 2.7 g   **Protein** 0.4 g

Tip: Freezing is a great way to store your excess rhubarb! Just chop the stalks into small pieces and spread onto a parchment paper-lined baking sheet in a single layer. Freeze until hard, then transfer to freezer-safe bags or containers.

Rhubarb Strawberry

Growing up in Alaska, we couldn't be picky about the fruits and veggies we got. Like mango? I'll spend my $7 elsewhere, thank you. But in the land of the midnight sun, there are some plants that flourish. And those plants, you learn to love them. Case in point: rhubarb. Ultra-tart and bitter on its own, rhubarb blends perfectly with sweet strawberries. But for the days that are too hot to turn on the oven for classic strawberry rhubarb crisp . . . we popsicle.

difficulty   **Yields: about 2 cups, 8 (2-oz.) pops**

1½ cups quartered strawberries (fresh or frozen)
1½ cups rhubarb (fresh or frozen)
¼ cup honey or sugar
2 Tbsp water or orange juice
Pinch of salt

1. Add all ingredients to a medium saucepan and set over medium heat. Cook uncovered, stirring occasionally, until the fruits have mostly broken down, about 10 minutes. It should have a runny jelly-like consistency. If it's too watery, continue cooking with the lid off to let the moisture evaporate out.

2. Spoon into molds, leaving a little space at the top for them to expand. Insert sticks and freeze until hard (at least 4 hours).

3. Run the mold under warm water for a few seconds to loosen them up, then remove from the mold.

Calories 47   **Fat** 0.1 g   **Saturated Fat** 0 g   **Carbs** 12.2 g   **Fiber** 1.1 g   **Sugar** 10.5 g   **Protein** 0.5 g

Roasted Peaches and Cream

If you've ever had the perfect peach—I'm talking the juicy, ultra-sweet peaches that taste straight out of Georgia—then you understand the utter disappointment of a bad peach. But by roasting them in the oven with a drizzle of honey and pinch of salt, bad peaches become soft and caramelized (and good peaches become, well, perfection).

difficulty 🍦🍦🍦   **Yields: about 2 cups, 8 (2-oz.) pops**

1 heaping cup chopped ripe peaches (3–4 medium peaches)
3 Tbsp honey, divided
Pinch of salt
1 cup plain Greek yogurt
½ tsp vanilla extract

1. Preheat oven to 375° F. Set chopped peaches onto a parchment paper-lined baking sheet and drizzle with 1 tablespoon honey and a pinch of salt. Toss around to combine and spread into a single layer. Bake for 20 to 25 minutes, or until tender and juicy. Allow to cool on the sheet for 20 minutes.

2. Meanwhile combine yogurt, vanilla extract, and remaining 2 tablespoons honey.

3. Spoon some of the yogurt mixture into each mold, followed by a spoonful of peaches, followed by more yogurt. Continue adding each, in alternating layers, until you've used it all. Gently tap the pop mold on the counter to remove air pockets. Insert sticks and freeze until hard (at least 4 hours).

4. Run the mold under warm water for a few seconds to loosen them up, then remove from the mold.

Calories 74   **Fat** 1.9 g   **Saturated Fat** 1.1 g   **Carbs** 13.7 g   **Fiber** 0.9 g   **Sugar** 13.6 g   **Protein** 1.7 g

Simply Strawberry

When I polled our blog reader to see what people's favorite pop flavors were, I almost unanimously heard back "red." Which I'm taking the liberty of translating to mean "strawberry." Because there's nothing more summery than picking too many strawberries than you know what to do with and finding yourself working them into every recipe you make. Enter, these ice pops.

difficulty   **Yields: about 2 cups, 8 (2-oz.) pops**

2 heaping cups quartered strawberries (fresh or frozen and thawed)
¼ cup honey or sugar
2 Tbsp lemon juice (1 lemon)

1. Combine all ingredients in a blender until smooth.

2. Pour into molds, leaving a little space at the top for them to expand. Insert sticks and freeze until hard (at least 4 hours).

3. Run the mold under warm water for a few seconds to loosen them up, then remove from the mold.

Calories 37   **Fat** 0.1 g   **Saturated Fat** 0 g   **Carbs** 9.3 g   **Fiber** 0.8 g   **Sugar** 8.2 g   **Protein** 0.3 g

Tip: Make this recipe vegan by using aquafaba (the juice in a can of chickpeas) instead of the egg whites. Simply replace the eggs with the juice from one 15-oz. can of chickpeas, whipping until you get stiff peaks.

S'mores

The single best thing about summers in Alaska (aside from the camping, fishing, and 22 hours of sunlight) is the bonfires. Truck beds loaded up with the essentials, we drive out into the sticks looking for the perfect place to build our fire. And everyone has their thing they would bring. One brings the wood pallets, another the spiked lemonade and lawn chairs. And me? I bring the makings for s'mores. These popsicles take everything that make s'mores the perfect summer dessert and make them fit for even the hottest of days.

difficulty   **Yields: 1½ cups, 6 (2-oz.) pops**

Chocolate popsicle base
 1 (14-oz.) can coconut milk
 ½ cup unsweetened cocoa powder
 2–4 Tbsp maple syrup or honey, to taste
 1 tsp vanilla extract
 Pinch of salt

Marshmallow graham cracker topping
 3 large eggs, whites only (room
   temperature for best results)
 ¼ tsp cream of tartar
 ½ cup sugar
 ½ teaspoon vanilla extract
 4 graham crackers, crumbled into crumbs

1. Combine base ingredients in a blender until evenly mixed.

2. Pour into molds, leaving a little space at the top. Insert sticks and freeze until hard (at least 4 hours).

3. Just before removing pops from the freezer, make your marshmallow topping. Add egg whites and cream of tartar to a clean bowl and begin to whip with a standing or hand mixer. When eggs start to become foamy, gradually add in sugar. Continue whipping to stiff peaks (when you remove the beaters from the bowl, the egg whites should stand straight up without folding over). Add vanilla extract and beat in very briefly.

4. Run the mold under warm water for a few seconds, then remove popsicles from the mold. Let them soften at room temperature for a few minutes, then spoon on the marshmallow coating and sprinkle with graham cracker crumbs.

5. Use a kitchen torch to lightly toast the meringue. Serve immediately or return pops to the freezer on a parchment paper-lined plate until ready to eat (best when served on the same day).

Calories 215   **Fat** 11.5 g   **Saturated Fat** 9.2 g   **Carbs** 28 g   **Fiber** 3.5 g   **Sugar** 18.3 g   **Protein** 4.8 g

Strawberries and Cream

Can we take a moment to remember the pink and white swirled hard candies previously known as Creme Savers? Because what happened to those? One moment I was hunting for them in the hymnal racks of the pews in my childhood church, and the next I was an adult coming to the realization that I haven't set eyes on them in years. And while I'm still not sure how to find these creamy flavor bomb candies, these pops bring back the nostalgia.

difficulty

Yields: about 2 cups, 8 (2-oz.) pops

1½ cups quartered strawberries (fresh or frozen and thawed)
4 Tbsp honey or sugar, divided
1 cup plain Greek yogurt
½ tsp vanilla extract

1. Blend together strawberries and 2 tablespoons honey until smooth. In a separate bowl, stir together remaining 2 tablespoons of honey, yogurt, and vanilla extract.

2. Spoon a bit of the strawberry mixture into each mold, followed by a spoonful of the yogurt mixture. Continue adding each, in alternating layers, until you've used it all, leaving a little space at the top for them to expand. Insert sticks and freeze until hard (at least 4 hours).

3. Run the mold under warm water for a few seconds to loosen them up, then remove from the mold.

Calories 69   **Fat** 1.8 g   **Saturated Fat** 1.1 g   **Carbs** 12.6 g   **Fiber** 0.6 g   **Sugar** 11.9 g   **Protein** 1.3 g

Tip: *This recipe works well with just about any berry, though you may need to adjust the honey if using tart berries.*

Tip: Many breakfast cereals are sprinkled with freeze dried red berries, like Special K Red Berries, and various granola mixes. Pick out a handful to help give this classic pop its signature coating.

Strawberry Shortcake

Pavlov's dogs responded to a bell by drooling. We humans have a similar response. When we hear an ice cream truck, we involuntarily drop what we're doing and make a dash for the road. Classical conditioning, friends, we can't fight it (trust me, I almost got a minor in psychology). And while some people lose themselves in the dazzling menu of ice pop-ssibilites, my sights are always set on one—the crunchy on the outside, creamy on the inside, heaven on a stick Strawberry Shortcake Popsicles.

difficulty    **Yields: about 2 cups, 8 (2-oz.) pops**

2 cups quartered strawberries (fresh or frozen and thawed)
1 banana
½ cup milk (can substitute canned coconut milk for richer pops)
2 Tbsp honey
½ cup corn flake cereal
4 Tbsp freeze-dried strawberries
1 Tbsp unsalted butter, melted

1. Blend together strawberries, banana, milk, and honey until smooth.

2. Pour into molds, leaving a little space at the top for them to expand. Insert sticks and freeze until hard (at least 4 hours).

3. Crush corn flakes and freeze-dried strawberries (using either a rolling pin or by blitzing in the food processor into a fine crumb). Stir to combine crushed corn flakes, crushed strawberries, and melted butter.

4. Run the mold under warm water for a few seconds to loosen popsicles up, then remove from the mold.

5. Line a plate with parchment paper. Coat each pop in the crumb coating (this is easier if you let the pops warm up just a touch so the outsides are soft, or if you drizzle them with additional honey). Set on the prepared plate and return to the freezer for at least 10 minutes, then serve.

Calories 70   **Fat** 2 g   **Saturated Fat** 1.1 g   **Carbs** 15.7 g   **Fiber** 1.4 g   **Sugar** 10.3 g   **Protein** 1.2 g

Tip: For added natural sweetness, roast rather than boil your sweet potato chunks before blending them. Toss them in flavorless oil and bake for 30 minutes at 450° F, flipping occasionally to evenly cook.

Sweet Potato Pie

Sweet Potato Pie is Pumpkin Pie's fraternal twin. Everyone says they look the same, but Sweet Potato Pie has a thick southern drawl that makes her cozier and sweeter somehow. And as sisters do, she likes to steal Pumpkin Pie's clothes, in this case the coveted pumpkin pie spice.

difficulty 🍦🍦🍦   **Yields: about 2 cups, 8 (2-oz.) pops**

1 cup peeled and roughly chopped sweet potato (about 1 potato)
1 cup canned coconut milk
¼ cup maple syrup
1 Tbsp pumpkin pie spice (or 1½ tsp ground cinnamon, ¼ tsp ground cloves,
  ¼ tsp ground ginger)
½ tsp vanilla extract
Pinch of salt
Optional cream layer: ¼ cup canned coconut milk + 1 Tbsp maple syrup

1. Add sweet potato to a pot of boiling water and cook for 10 minutes, or until potatoes are fork tender.

2. Combine sweet potato with the coconut milk, maple syrup, pumpkin pie spice, vanilla, and salt in a blender until smooth.

3. Pour into molds, leaving a little space at the top for them to expand (leave more space if you want to add the optional cream layer). Insert sticks and freeze until hard (at least 4 hours).

4. If you want the cream layer, stir to combine coconut milk and maple syrup, then pour into the remaining space of each mold after the sweet potato layer has frozen completely. Return to the freezer until frozen.

5. Run the mold under warm water for a few seconds to loosen them up, then remove from the mold.

Calories 113   **Fat** 5.1 g   **Saturated Fat** 3.6 g   **Carbs** 15.6 g   **Fiber** 0.8 g   **Sugar** 8.6 g   **Protein** 0.8 g

Tip: Replace 2 Tbsp of the coffee with 2 Tbsp of coffee liqueur (like Kahlua) for a boozy hint.

Tiramisu

A cup of coffee and a sweet treat is one of my favorite ways to end a night, with the bitterness of the coffee bringing out the sweetness of the dessert. And any dish that manages to put all of that into one bite is an instant winner. I'm talking tiramisu. These pops replace the fat-laden mascarpone traditionally found in tiramisu with a blend of yogurt and cream cheese. All the rich, creaminess without all the guilt (so, I call seconds!)

difficulty    **Yields: about 2 cups, 8 (2-oz.) pops**

1 heaping cup roughly torn angel food cake or ladyfingers
¼ cup coffee, chilled
¾ cup plain Greek yogurt
¾ cup cream cheese
2 Tbsp packed brown sugar (can substitute no-calorie sweetener)
Optional: unsweetened cocoa powder

1. Tear angel food cake into roughly ½-inch chunks and set them in a small bowl. Drizzle coffee over chunks to mostly cover them.

2. In a small bowl, stir together yogurt, cream cheese, and brown sugar.

3. Add a spoonful of the yogurt mixture to each mold, followed by a few pieces of cake. Be sure to push the cake into the yogurt to remove air pockets. Keep adding yogurt and cake, in alternating layers, until the molds are full. Insert sticks and freeze until hard (at least 4 hours).

4. Run the mold under warm water for a few seconds to loosen them up, then remove from the mold. Optionally dust each popsicle with cocoa powder before serving.

Calories 115   **Fat** 8.9 g   **Saturated Fat** 5.6 g   **Carbs** 6.2 g   **Fiber** 0.1 g   **Sugar** 3.7 g   **Protein** 2.7 g

Upside-Down Pineapple

If you've ever made pineapple upside-down cake, you'll know that moment of suspense and awe as you flip the cake tin over and lift up to reveal a golden dome of pineapple, cherry, cakey deliciousness. Layered with the naturally bright colors of pineapple and cherry, pulling these ice pops out of the mold has a similar effect (minus the insulin spike, sugar crash, and having to, ya know, bake a whole cake).

difficulty | Yields: about 2 cups, 8 (2-oz.) pops

2 cups chopped pineapple, divided
½ cup + 2 Tbsp plain Greek yogurt, divided
1 cup pitted cherries (fresh or frozen and thawed)

1. Finely chop ½ cup of the pineapple and spoon into the bottom of each ice pop well. Blend the remaining pineapple with ½ cup yogurt and pour into the molds, filling them each about ⅔ full.

2. Rinse out your blender then add remaining 2 tablespoons of yogurt and cherries. Blend until smooth, then spoon into the remaining space of each mold.

3. Use a popsicle stick or spoon to push the cherry layer into the pineapple layer, creating rough swirls. Insert sticks and freeze until hard (at least 4 hours).

4. Run the mold under warm water for a few seconds to loosen them up, then remove from the mold.

Calories 48   **Fat** 1.3 g   **Saturated Fat** 0.8 g   **Carbs** 9 g   **Fiber** 0.9 g   **Sugar** 6.9 g   **Protein** 1.2 g

Tip: Between the chocolate coating and chopped almonds, these pops can get a bit messy! Best to eat them outside or over a plate.

Vanilla Cherry

Imagine a parallel universe where chocolate-covered cherries are healthy and easy to make and you can maybe even have them for breakfast. Well, we're far along enough in this book for you to know that the parallel universe = popsicles (and that we have zero problems with you enjoying them for breakfast).

difficulty

Yields: about 2 cups, 8 (2-oz.) pops

1 cup plain Greek yogurt
1 Tbsp honey
½ tsp vanilla extract
1 heaping cup pitted cherries (fresh or frozen and thawed)
½ cup dark or milk chocolate (chips or a roughly chopped bar)
¼ cup chopped almonds

1. In a small bowl, combine yogurt, honey, and vanilla. In a food processor, blitz the cherries until fairly smooth.

2. Add a spoonful of yogurt to each mold, followed by a spoonful of cherry. Keep adding yogurt and cherry, in alternating layers, until the molds are full. Use a popsicle stick or spoon to gently swirl a few times to combine the layers. Insert sticks and freeze until hard (at least 4 hours).

3. Before removing popsicles from the freezer, melt the chocolate by adding it to a heat-resistant bowl. Bring a pot of water to a boil and set the bowl of chocolate over the boiling water (just above the water, not submerged). Stir constantly until most of the chocolate is melted. Remove the bowl from over the steam and continue to stir until chocolate has all melted.

4. Remove popsicles from the freezer and run the mold under warm water for a few seconds to loosen them up. Remove each from the mold, drizzle with chocolate, and quickly sprinkle with chopped almonds.

Calories 119   **Fat** 6.4 g   **Saturated Fat** 3.4 g   **Carbs** 13.3 g   **Fiber** 1.1 g   **Sugar** 11.2 g   **Protein** 2.8 g

Tip: The sweetened condensed milk traditionally found in Vietnamese Iced Coffee is replaced with cashew cream in these healthified pops. If you're feeling indulgent, simply combine 1½ cups of chilled coffee with ½ cup sweetened condensed milk and freeze into pops!

Vietnamese Iced Coffee

I expected my favorite foods from my my trip to Southeast Asia to be pho, spring rolls, Bánh mi, or at least something of the sort. So I slurped down pho for breakfast in Ho Chi Minh and whipped up fresh spring rolls at a cooking school in Chiang Mai. But my favorite flavor to come out of the trip? Vietnamese iced coffee! A sock-rocking combination of strong iced coffee and sweetened condensed milk, so refreshingly delicious that when a savvy street monkey from the primate-run town of Lopburi jumped on my arm to take it from me, I almost fought him off (ultimately accepting defeat and buying another cup at the next street vendor).

difficulty   **Yields: a little less than 2 cups, 6–8 (2-oz.) pops**

1 cup raw cashews
1½ cups coffee, chilled, divided
¼–½ cup maple syrup or honey, to taste
2 tsp vanilla extract
Pinch of salt

1. To prep, soak cashews in a bowl of water in the refrigerator for at least 4 hours. Meanwhile, brew coffee and set in the refrigerator to chill.

2. Drain water from cashews and combine nuts in a blender with the maple syrup, vanilla, and salt until smooth and creamy, about 2 minutes. Add more or less maple syrup to suit your taste.

3. Evenly distribute 1 cup of the coffee into the bottom of each popsicle mold. Evenly spoon in the cashew cream, then top off with the remaining coffee. Use a popsicle stick or spoon to loosely blend the cashew cream with the coffee. Insert sticks and freeze until hard (at least 4 hours).

4. Run the mold under warm water for a few seconds to loosen them up, then remove from the mold.

Calories 114   **Fat** 6.5 g   **Saturated Fat** 1 g   **Carbs** 11.2 g   **Fiber** 0.5 g   **Sugar** 7 g   **Protein** 2.6 g

Wake Me Up

Who's to say you can't have popsicles in the morning? Especially when they're loaded with all the makin's of a well-rounded breakfast! With fruit, oats, Greek yogurt, and coffee, these pops have what you need to get from zero to fully-functioning adult in minutes.

difficulty   **Yields: about 2 cups, 8 (2-oz.) pops**

1 banana
1 cup coffee, chilled
½ cup plain Greek yogurt
¼ cup oats (rolled or instant)
2–4 Tbsp honey or maple syrup, to taste
2 Tbsp almond butter (or your favorite nut butter)

1. Combine all ingredients in a blender until smooth, adding more or less honey to suit your taste.

2. Pour into molds, leaving a little space at the top for them to expand. Insert sticks and freeze until hard (at least 4 hours).

3. Run the mold under warm water for a few seconds to loosen them up, then remove from the mold.

Calories 79   **Fat** 3.2 g   **Saturated Fat** 0.8 g   **Carbs** 11.9 g   **Fiber** 1.1 g   **Sugar** 8.1 g   **Protein** 1.9 g

Tip: This recipe also works well with fresh strawberries! Just sub the watermelon for an equal amount of quartered strawberries.

Watermelon Daiquiri

A lot of people seem to think watermelon is the epitome of summer, but I beg to differ. I blame a childhood allergy to melons for my distaste towards the whole watermelon business. But as if we needed another reason to love coconut rum (see "Spring Break 2012" and "Piña Colada" pops on page 117), this sweet elixir got me over my aversion to watermelon real fast.

difficulty   **Yields: about 2 cups, 8 (2-oz.) pops**

2 heaping cups chopped watermelon, seeds removed
½ cup coconut rum (like Malibu)
2–4 Tbsp honey or sugar, to taste
2 Tbsp lime juice (1 lime)

1. Combine all ingredients in a blender until smooth, adding more or less honey to suit your taste. Strain through a fine sieve to remove seeds and fibers (the melon fibers tend to give an odd texture when frozen).

2. Pour into molds, leaving a little space at the top for them to expand. Freeze for 1 hour, until slushy, then stir each mold to equally disperse the alcohol and melon. Insert sticks and freeze until hard (at least 8 hours).

3. Run the mold under warm water for a few seconds to loosen them up, then remove from the mold.

Calories 60 **Fat** 0.1 g **Saturated Fat** 0 g **Carbs** 11.3 g **Fiber** 0.4 g **Sugar** 10 g **Alcohol** 2.5 g **Protein** 0.3 g

Tip: This mixture makes a killer cocktail. Chop and freeze the watermelon on a baking sheet (so they don't clump together), then blend them up with the rest of the ingredients (adding a splash of water if needed to get things moving).

Tip: If you notice your "watermelon seeds" sinking to the bottom, let the mixture freeze for about an hour, then use a spoon to stir them back up.

Watermelon Kiwi

Eating is a lot more visual than you would think. For example, when we taste juices that are redder than others, we tend to think they are sweeter. Even wine connoisseurs can be fooled. When white wines are dyed red, they are perceived as more fruity and full-bodied than the same white wine when it's tasted in its natural color. I guess what I'm saying is, ice pops that not only taste but also look like watermelon are bound to be the most watermelony pops . . . ever (#science).

difficulty **Yields: a bit over 2 cups, 8 (2-oz.) pops**

1 heaping cup chopped watermelon, seeds removed
½ cup quartered strawberries (fresh or frozen and thawed)
2 Tbsp honey, divided
1 Tbsp lemon juice (½ of a lemon)
Optional: handful of chocolate chips
¼ cup canned coconut milk
2 kiwis

1. Combine watermelon, strawberries, 1 tablespoon honey, and lemon juice in a blender until smooth. Strain through a fine sieve to remove seeds and fibers (the melon fibers tend to give an odd texture when frozen).

2. Pour evenly into molds, filling a little more than half of each well. Try not to spill the mixture on the sides of the molds, but simply wipe off with a paper towel if you do (we want tidy layers to show). Optionally sprinkle in a few chocolate chips to resemble seeds, gently pushing them deeper into the mixture using a popsicle stick. Cover with lid or aluminum foil (use foil if your popsicles sticks have a hard time standing upright), insert sticks, and freeze until hard (at least 4 hours).

3. Once watermelon layer is frozen, evenly top each with coconut milk. Return to freezer until frozen.

4. Spoon kiwi from the skin and blitz in a blender with the remaining tablespoon of honey. Top off each pop, and return to the freezer until frozen.

5. Run the mold under warm water for a few seconds to loosen them up, then remove from the mold.

Calories 59　　**Fat** 2.2 g　　**Saturated Fat** 1.8 g　　**Carbs** 10.2 g　　**Fiber** 1 g　　**Sugar** 8.4 g　　**Protein** 0.7 g

Yogurt Parfait

Smoothies were my gateway to popsicles. The beauty of smoothies is you can probably fashion some kind or another with whatever you happen to have in your kitchen. The same holds for ice pops! Case in point: these Yogurt Parfait Pops. You don't even need a mold to make these guys. Just stir fruit into small yogurt cups, top with granola (or any cereal), throw a stick in it, and freeze.

difficulty   **Yields: 6 pops**

6 small fruit-flavored yogurt cups (about 5.3 oz each)
½ cup fresh fruit of choice, finely chopped
¼ cup granola or breakfast cereal

1. Remove a spoonful of yogurt from each cup. Evenly distribute fruit into each cup and stir to combine. Top with granola or cereal.

2. Insert sticks and freeze until hard (at least 4 hours).

3. Run the yogurt containers under warm water for a few seconds to loosen them up, then remove pops.

Nutrition information will differ depending on the yogurt and fruit you use, but this is a rough indication.

Calories 109   **Fat** 4.1 g   **Saturated Fat** 1.7 g   **Carbs** 15.6 g   **Fiber** 1.2 g   **Sugar** 11.9 g   **Protein** 9.1 g

Tip: *If you don't have small yogurt cups, you can just as easily use a big tub of yogurt, put a stick in it, and make a GIANT yogurt pop . . . Jokes. Just use about 1½ cups yogurt and ½ cup fruit, spoon into ice pop molds, and top off with granola!*

Zucchini Bread

I'm not sure about the sanity of the person who first decided to put zucchini into a sweetened bread (likewise for carrots and cake), but a wonderful invention it was! And I'm sure some would also question the sanity of the person who thought zucchini in popsicles would be a good idea, but in a book of healthy pops from A to Z, the "Z" is a must (and with creamy coconut, nutty oats, an array of spices, and shredded zucchini, these pops are a must too!).

difficulty | **Yields: about 2 cups, 8 (2-oz.) pops**

1 cup canned coconut milk
½ cup oats (rolled or instant)
¼ cup honey or maple syrup
1 tsp vanilla extract
½ tsp ground cinnamon
¼ tsp ground cloves
¼ tsp ground nutmeg
Pinch of salt
1 cup shredded zucchini (you can leave the peel on)

1. Combine all ingredients except zucchini in a blender until smooth. Stir in shredded zucchini. Alternatively, blend zucchini in with all other ingredients to easily "hide" the zucchini.

2. Pour into molds, leaving a little space at the top for them to expand. Insert sticks and freeze until hard (at least 4 hours).

3. Run the mold under warm water for a few seconds to loosen them up, then remove from the mold.

Calories 125   **Fat** 7.6 g   **Saturated Fat** 6.4 g   **Carbs** 14.6 g   **Fiber** 1.5 g   **Sugar** 10.1 g   **Protein** 1.6 g

TASTE TESTER APPROVED

Each recipe in this book was rigorously tested and refined in *real* homes by *real* people. Tremendous thanks therefore go to the dedicated, popsicle-loving taste testers of this book:

Sarah Svedin and the Svedin kids, who helped test and tailor so many recipes to be kid-approved (even a few that have hidden veggies!).

Jenn Anderson and her 1½-year-old daughter, Luellyn; Jenn's photo updates of Luellyn loving the pops motivated me to keep churning out batch after batch.

Sandy Axelrod (of TheTravelingLocavores.com), who enthusiastically took on many recipes, often serving them to her popsicle-holic husband.

Blaire Wikoff (of MissFingerFoodie.com), who took her passion for clean eating to bring new inspiration and life into the pops she tested.

Karen and Eastlyn Fell, two old friends who, despite living in less-than-balmy Alaska, tried out many popsicle recipes.

Sarah Frank Roberts (of FranklyEntertaining.com), yet another Alaska-based taster who was the guinea pig for many of the more unique recipes, like Igloo Baked Alaska and Eat Your Protein (with cottage cheese!).

My own Aunt Linda along with Marissa and Jared, who jumped in to help and gathered loads of critical Bostonian feedback after serving a few batches at a family reunion.

Leona Konkel (of FoodsILike.net), who relentlessly helped perfect one of my favorite recipes in the book, Marshmallow Coconut Creme.

Elizabeth Waterson (of ConfessionsOfABakingQueen.com), who could be better known as the "Poptail Queen" after helping to test out a few of the boozy pops in this book.

Sally Taber, who provided the highly coveted "Kid Seal of Approval" on a few pops (especially the Dulce Date Leche!).

Rénana Spiegel Levkovich (of Renanas.kitchen), who gave her unique popsicle perspective all the way from Israel.

Heather Reed, who enthusiastically jumped in late into the summer, quickly testing and providing thoughtful tips that ultimately resulted in even tastier pops.

Shannon Emery (of PassMeSomeTasty.com), who used her love of healthy, down-to-earth food to help develop the recipes into wholesome treats that her whole family would love.

Mary Stephens (on Facebook as The Creative Saver) who provided a dairy-free perspective, thoughtfully testing pops with her husband.

Michelle Savage (of GreenAisleWellness.com), who used her background as an integrative nutrition health coach and healthy cookbook author to support the writing of this book.

THANK YOU

To Jor, the tulip-man, who despite not actually being a lover of popsicles, tasted and critically evaluated every ambiguous mixture and frozen pop I held in your face. For your patience when dinner became an afterthought in lieu of making popsicles, and for your refusal to let me give up on my wildest ideas (except cabbage pops, thank you for letting me give up on that one).

To my parents, for your unending support when I left a "real" job to pursue my passions in food. For being my very first blog readers, for proofreading every page of this book, and for eagerly testing the Darling Lemon Thyme pops again and again (and again).

To my sister, for letting me wear your favorite white shirt and playing my photographer extraordinaire as I ate a rapidly melting fuschia popsicle on the sunshiney beaches of Hawaii (and for generally being the sunshiniest person I know).

To my incredible editor, Leah, for your warm enthusiasm and support from an ocean away. And to the rest of the Skyhorse Publishing team for making this crazy thing called my first cookbook possible.

And to my Live Eat Learn readers, who support and inspire me, and ultimately made this book possible.

ABOUT THE AUTHOR

Sarah Bond is the recipe developer and author behind the food blog, Live Eat Learn, where she uses her backgrounds in nutrition and sensory science to create unique and healthy(ish) vegetarian recipes. Her insatiable case of the travel bug led her to move to the Netherlands, where she currently lives with her "tulip-man." When she's not exploring new ingredients in the kitchen, you can catch her adventuring near and far, usually in the name of food.

INDEX

CONVERSION CHART

METRIC AND IMPERIAL CONVERSIONS
(These conversions are rounded for convenience)

Ingredient	Cups/Tablespoons/ Teaspoons	Ounces	Grams/Milliliters
Fruit, dried	1 cup	4 ounces	120 grams
Fruits or veggies, chopped	1 cup	5 to 7 ounces	145 to 200 grams
Fruits or veggies, puréed	1 cup	8.5 ounces	245 grams
Honey, maple syrup, or corn syrup	1 tablespoon	0.75 ounce	20 grams
Liquids: cream, milk, water, or juice	1 cup	8 fluid ounces	240 milliliters
Salt	1 teaspoon	0.2 ounces	6 grams
Spices: cinnamon, cloves, ginger, or nutmeg (ground)	1 teaspoon	0.2 ounce	5 grams
Sugar, brown, firmly packed	1 cup	7 ounces	200 grams
Sugar, white	1 cup/1 tablespoon	7 ounces/0.5 ounce	200 grams/12.5 grams
Vanilla extract	1 teaspoon	0.2 ounce	4 grams